From Alsace to Yorkshire

The Making of a Passion

Lionel Strub

Fisher King Publishing

Published by
Fisher King Publishing
The Studio
Arthington Lane
Pool-in-Wharfedale
LS21 1JZ
England

From Alsace to Yorkshire

ISBN 978-1-906377-47-2

Design by Sam Richardson
Photography by Jonathan Ogden

Contents

I believe passion is probably one of the most important dimensions of the human composition, without passion we are left without those dreams and aspirations that keep us going.

In Memory of
Gordon Harrison

Foreword

I was extremely pleased when Lionel asked me to write the forward for this, his first book. It is such an honour to be asked because, knowing Lionel as I do, I was already aware that this book is intensely personal to him. Alsace to Yorkshire is more than a cookbook, it is Lionel's journey, a journey with which any chef or restaurateur will identify, I certainly did.

The Celebrity chef may have thrust food onto our TV screens and into miles of print giving the illusion that a chef's life is glamorous, cool and, easy. Thankfully, Lionel blows that myth well out of the water in the telling of his roller-coaster journey and the perfectly described hard-work and daily grind of the hospitality industry. The precarious nature of the restaurant business which has you on a high one moment and penniless the next has happened to many restaurateurs but few talk about it and those that do rarely do so with the brutal honesty shown here. If cheffing and the restaurant business is so risky then why does anyone ever do it? Read this book for the answer (the clues – Lionel's passion for cooking, love of food and sheer determination).

Every young chef should read this book before they embark on a career in cooking, if they are chasing glamour Lionel will certainly put them right.

I first met Lionel when he arrived at Harvey Nichols one September evening for the finals of the Chef of the Year Competition. I had devised the event with the Yorkshire Agricultural Society to raise the profile of the food and cooking in the county. We had been inundated with entries and whittling them down to the final four was an arduous task with the high standards on offer. The finished dish though important was not the only criteria we judges were looking at, it was the professionalism and approach of the chef to their work and from the get-go Lionel shone. He

arrived early, he was well prepared, he worked quietly and assiduously, and his food wowed the judges. He was our first and to this day remains one of the best chefs to enter the competition.

I have since followed his career through the glory, the hard times and phoenix-like rising at the delightful Mirabelle Restaurant in Harrogate. Now, having read this book it is clear to me where his tenacity, even in the darkest hours, comes from and why it is I love his food so much. It is because he pours his passion into every dish, cherishes every opportunity to prove that the unteachable young boy did good, and he works like a demon.

Lionel's success however is not just his dogged determination, he is also a very talented chef with an enviable ability to fuse the cooking of two, vital, lively areas, Yorkshire and Alsace. Each has their own culinary identity yet Lionel has taken the best of each and let them shine individually as well as together. As the wealth of recipes in the book shows Lionel has held on to his roots whist embracing those of his 'new' home. Alsace's loss was certainly Yorkshire's gain.

Elaine Lemm
Food and drink journalist
Author of The Great Book of Yorkshire Pudding
and of The Great Book Of Rhubarb

THE GREAT BOOK OF

rhubarb

ELAINE LEMM

THE GREAT BOOK OF

yorkshire pudding

ELAINE LEMM

FOREWORD BY ROSEMARY SHRAGER

Introduction

From Alsace to Yorkshire is a blend of recipes and autobiographic stories from a troubled child to a successful and award winning chef and restaurateur. This is the challenging journey of Lionel Strub through life from France to England, from Alsace to Yorkshire.

Classically trained chef Lionel Strub graduated from Ecole Hoteliere de Strasbourg in 1982. From the age of six Lionel worked in his Grandfather's bakery. It was there that Lionel drew inspiration and belief in simplicity and quality of ingredients. After graduating, Lionel spent three years at Le Restaurant des Vannes in Liverdun, an acclaimed two Michelin star restaurant with head chef Jean Pierre Cotard.

After a year in Germany during his national service, Lionel worked in restaurants across Europe and the UK.

After twenty five years in England, Lionel is now an award winning chef and restaurateur running Mirabelle Restaurant in Harrogate, North Yorkshire. Lionel has developed an unusual and creative combination of modern French and British cookery.

The Making of a Passion

There is an old French proverb that goes – "Il faut casser le noyau pour avoir l'amande" which translates "You need to break the shell to have the almond." To have got to where I am today feels like a very long and often painful journey and here are just some parts of the story followed by some of the recipes that reflect turning points in my life.

From Pillar to Post

I was born in Eastern France in June1964 in what was a small, yet quickly growing, town called Nancy in the region called Alsace Lorraine. My mum was a young nineteen year old student nurse at the local hospital. I think my dad was a bus driver, but he was also married to someone else and did not hang around once he found out mum was pregnant. To this day my mum doesn't often speak about him and he never got in touch with me so I know little more.

In 1964 no real help was given to single mothers. It was clear to mum that she could not both work and look after me. So the first few years of my life were spent in foster care after which I ended up being passed around family friends and people I barely knew.

I still vividly remember staying in a home where I had to eat alone in a different room away from everyone else simply because I wasn't considered part of the family. I didn't seem to fit in anywhere or with anyone. This went on for some time and I became very unsettled, over-active and badly behaved. This was reflected in my early school years which were nothing short of a living nightmare.

Then at the age of eight my Grandma decided enough was enough and undertook to look after me rather than seeing me being part of a game of 'pass the parcel'.

Grandma had a nice house with a garden which when I returned some years later I was surprised to find was quite small. My recollection was of a field the size of a football pitch!

Every morning we would go to the 'lavoir public', the public laundry. This was next to the river Meutre and consisted of several stone cubicles with a wooden board. No one in rural France had a washing machine so women would meet there every day to do their washing. I remember this being such an exciting time. The place was buzzing with noise, children playing and women working together, chatting and helping each other.

Women were very hard working, an after-effect of the Second World War when they had no choice but to keep the country afloat whilst their men were away fighting. Life at Grandma's was peaceful and stable and I have fond memories of my Grandma really loving me, and showing she really cared. For me this was the very best of times. I knew I was loved, I had friends and I was happy. I remember a strong sense of community and more importantly the comfort of feeling I belonged. I remember very little of my Granddad.

I stayed with Grandma for four years until I was twelve when she sadly died of liver cancer. She wrote me a letter a few days before she passed away hoping that when she left hospital we would go and get an ice cream and life would be great again. I still treasure that letter she wrote all those years ago, together with her wedding ring which I have kept all this time for my own daughter's wedding day.

Whilst I will never forget the happiness of those four years living at my Grandma's, it is tinged with a deep sense of sadness that she never had the chance to see the difference her commitment, love and affection made in making me the person I am today.

So with Grandma gone, in 1976, at the age of twelve, I moved back to be with my mum. She had recently become engaged to a handsome lorry driver and was soon married. Together they had three more children, my sister Isabelle and two brothers, Dominique and Sylvain.

For me it meant yet another complete change of home, family and school. Despite a life of constant change and rarely staying in any place for any length of time I have never got used to it. To this day the fear of not belonging painfully haunts me whenever change is on the horizon.

My school years were highly unproductive to the point that my teacher suggested I be placed in a school for those with special needs. After 3 months at the special school it was decided it was not the place for me and they moved me back to mainstream school but with little expectation of my doing much better.

Looking back I think it could well be that I suffered with ADHD (Attention Deficit and Hyperactivity Disorder), but that kind of thing wasn't recognised or understood when I was a child. My behaviour clearly irritated the teachers and led to some very difficult school years with few happy memories. In all my years at school there was little evidence I would ever concentrate or become studious in any way. As a child, the notion that one-day I would become a college lecturer, a successful restaurateur, or publish a book, would have been considered by most to be foolish fantasy.

My Grandma and my Mum were great cooks and also made some amazing jam. Most of my recipes come from my Grandma and I have her little book of jams and chutneys which I still use today. Whenever I returned home, lentil, sausage and sour cream was the dish Mum cooked for me, and still to this day it's the first meal eat when I visit her evoking those early memories. It was at the age of six I discovered that above all else I too wanted to cook. One Sunday morning my sister Isabelle was Christened. Instead of spending my time joining the rest of the screaming kids running around the tray of jam sandwiches I stayed in the kitchen totally mesmerised by the chefs busily preparing the food for the family celebration. From that day I felt destined and above all else determined to cook.

From School to Work

At the age of 15 I left school to take on an apprenticeship at 'Le Gran Cerf restaurant in Luneville, a town 60 miles from Strasbourg. Whilst initially this may have seemed like a dream come true, it was a very hard and frustrating time. I lived on the premises and before starting work I had to collect and bring wood for the ovens and then spent the day washing up, all for just £15 a week. In the second year things did gradually begin to improve when the new apprentice arrived and took over the menial tasks. At last I started to cook. I worked with the chefs all day learning the tricks of the trade. During break times and days off I spent time with the butcher who taught me how to make rillettes, terrines, pates and sausages. I still use many of the recipes and methods I learnt at that time and some of them appear in this book.

Suddenly I had a hunger to learn. The one at the bottom of the class throughout my school years, I had at last discovered a vocation worth working and studying for. I worked six days a week, two of which were supposed to be spent at college, but my chef was always reluctant to let me go. As a result my tutor threatened to throw me out of the course if I didn't attend college regularly. I was caught between the two and though it was tough I wanted to devour everything that was on offer.

Eventually I qualified as a chef. I had made it, I found the kitchen to be a place where I belonged and was happy. Cooking had become my saviour. Every day was different and for the first time I had a positive channel that others respected for my never-ending energy.

After three years at 'Le Gran Cerf' I moved on to 'Le Val Fleurie' - a Michelin Star restaurant in Liverdun, under head chef Jean Pierre Cotard. It was there that I discovered a new level where cooking was so much more than a job, more a way of living, a driving passion. The amount of time spent preparing the food, the obsessive attention to the smallest detail, and the way by which we cooked was simply breathtaking and demanded everything I had to give. I had no idea where it would lead, and didn't really care; I was caught up in the passion and all I knew was that this was the path that everything within me had to follow.

I was at 'Le Val Fleurie' for two years successfully working my way up to Sous Chef. Many years after I left, the owner Madam Limonge, told my mum that if ever I needed to return, a job would always be made available for me.

The Chef at 'Le Val Fleurie' was very strict, some would say a tyrant. On one occasion I left the fryer on after lunch by mistake, and when I returned for evening service he took my hand and dipped my fingers in the hot fat. The painful burns resulted in being off work for two weeks.

Jean Pierre was indisputably a hard man with a very 'old school' outlook, but he has now held a Michelin Star for twenty years and that is a very rare and remarkable achievement. He would purposely develop some of his recipes after everyone had left at night so that we could never know the exact ingredients. However, his memory wasn't brilliant, so he had a book in which he detailed all his recipes kept hidden in the napkin cupboard. I eventually found where it was concealed and photocopied the whole book before I left. Sorry Jean Pierre, now you know!

At twenty I left to do my national service based at Speyer, a little town 20 miles from Stuttgart. After two months training I was moved to Berlin where we used to cook for 2000 hungry soldiers. No thought of Michelin Stars in that kitchen. We almost cooked 24 hours a day to keep the garrison fed and happy.

The last five months there were quite different when my captain learnt that I had previously worked in a Michelin Star restaurant. I was quickly detailed to become what felt like his personal slave! When we did military exercises in the Black Forest I went out with my bayonet in search of wild crepe and girolle mushrooms using my uniform helmet as a basket. I would cook dinner for the captain and his fellow officers, and once he was drunk enough I was thankfully released from duty.

Unlike many, I actually enjoyed my time in the army. The security and discipline suited me. Having worked in very strict kitchens at the beck and call of eccentric superiors it didn't really feel all that different to me. Others really suffered because life in the army was so different to the comfortable cocoon of their lives back home.

After the army I spent two years working in kitchens in the south of France during the summer season and ski resorts during the winter. The money here was good, but so too were the parties, and my mum would usually have to give me the train fare to visit home.

From France to England

I moved to Britain in September 1986 with no cash and no real idea of how things would shape up.

I began by working in a busy brasserie in London's Brompton Road serving meals all day seven days a week. It truly was non-stop with an incredible turn-over and sometimes getting through the week was just a matter of survival.

Back then Britain was not renowned for its breadth of cuisine. Apart from a few French restaurants serving Boeuf Bourguignon, forever full Italian pizzerias and of course curry houses the British seemed to stay with what they knew. However, at that time chefs like Gary Rhodes, Gordon Ramsay and Marco Pierre White were coming onto the scene and British restaurants began to make a significant change.

Food in England in the late eighties started to become fashionable and more and more chefs became TV stars, restaurants started to be full every night. Dining and entertaining became a normal and regular part of social life.

British cuisine has now grown to be some of the best in the world, colourful and multicultural, with a vast range of quality products grown in the UK. The high standard of restaurants with familiar top chefs has firmly placed British food on the world stage. Some of the most celebrated French chefs like Joel Robuchon, Helen Daroze and Alain Ducasse now have restaurants in London, something that would not have been imagined when I first arrived in England in the mid-nineteen eighties.

And now it is that London has more Michelin Star restaurants than Paris - that's some progress in such a short time.

As in main land Europe, dining out in this country has become much more of a social occasion. The UK has caught up with the rest of Europe when it comes to socialising over dinner. To be a part of this social change of the last twenty five years has been an exciting opportunity.

From London to Yorkshire

After three years in London and Birmingham I moved to Yorkshire in 1989 to work at 'La Grillade' in Leeds, a great place where I learned so much. Not so much cooking this time, but the crucial skills of managing the kitchen, profit margins and pricing. La Grillade is still owned by Guy Martin Laval. A wine merchant by trade he is probably the most successful restaurateur in Yorkshire. I have a lot of respect for Mr Laval and many aspects of the way I run my restaurant owe a lot to my experience with him. Our paths sometimes still cross and it is always a pleasure to see him. I worked at La Grillade for seven years and left in 1996 to become a catering lecturer. This was another very difficult time in my personal life, my marriage was deteriorating by the day, and making little effort to rescue it, the result was divorce.

From Employee to Employer

After four years as a cooking lecturer in Leeds, recently divorced and once again penniless, I decided to open my own place. As funds were low I had to negotiate with the bank for a small loan of eight thousand pounds just to get me started. The HSBC bank manager at the time was Neil Ballantyne, a great man who believed in me and saw how passionate I was. With the loan safely in my account, in January 2001, the Fig and Fennel Delicatessen opened in Wetherby.

Starting any business is never easy, but I had no idea how much I would suffer before eventually tasting success. The lack of cash was a constant problem. After eighteen months I had amassed ten thousand pounds of debt on two credit cards just to keep the shop open. I had staff who rightly expected to be paid. Eventually I had to leave my flat as I couldn't afford to pay the rent and for eighteen months I slept in a sleeping bag in the shop. No one knew apart from my closest friends, my accountant and sadly my three children who saw their dad broke and homeless. We laugh about it now but it was horrid at the time.

In 2003 the shop really started to get busy and the business began to consistently break even. At last my luck seemed to be turning. The bank mentioned a grant for new businesses and I fitted the criteria. I applied and four weeks later I got a cheque for one thousand five hundred pounds to spend on the shop. It was to be the real beginning for Fig and Fennel. We bought twenty chairs, redesigned the premises and turned the place into both a coffee shop and delicatessen.

Wetherby's Fig and Fennel Coffee Shop was born. We started making a profit, life became easier and it even felt like success. At last I could move into a proper house with a proper bed! I was for the first time in my life both independent and self sufficient. After years of struggle, life was suddenly easier and it felt like everything I touched could be successful. Three years on and the coffee shop was full of regular customers, the delicatessen was actually making money and an outside catering business quickly developed. Within the next twelve months we had double the numbers of employees and the takings were rising on a weekly basis. My accountant was a happy man as business increased year on year for the next seven.

From Coffee Shop to Restaurant

With each year that passed I grew in confidence and when, in Autumn 2004, the adjoining shop closed I put in an offer. Four weeks later it was mine and Fennel Restaurant was launched less than two months after that.

Through the coffee shop and delicatessen we had established a core of local, loyal customers and a high reputation for quality so the restaurant naturally drew plenty of diners from week one.

Fennel was a small rectangular room with very little to commend it. The décor was simplistic and in fact the first food critic that visited us said, 'Mr Strub evidently has more feeling for the food he cooks than for his interior design.'

Well, Mrs Blake, I have to agree with you, but so many restaurants have beautiful interior design but little comes from the kitchen to compliment it. I knew where my priority lay and fortunately our customers seemed to agree.

The food was simple but cooked well. All the meat, poultry and fish we used at Fennel was sourced locally and we were very proud of the support for our local suppliers who were as passionate about their products as I was about cooking with them. Fennel on Bank Street was the first opportunity to cook as I really wanted, blending Alsace and Yorkshire cuisine in a creative and quite unique way.

Pie and peas, for example, is a staple and traditional Yorkshire meal which I enjoyed recreating by using a traditional Alsace duck confit, wild mushroom, foie gras and truffle wrapped in hot water pastry accompanied by mushy garden peas. Thus was born 'Posh Pie and Peas', one of many popular dishes that took diners on a culinary adventure.

Fennel had a strong team and I could not write about the success without mentioning Mark my Head Chef and Thomas my Shop and Restaurant Manager. They worked hard and long hours. I know my energy, impatience and mood swings can sometimes make me difficult to work with, but they were forgiving and very loyal workers and together we made a great team.

In 2005 readers of the Yorkshire Evening Post voted us one of the top five places to eat outside of Leeds City centre. As our reputation for quality grew so did our customer base which gave me the confidence to create more adventurous menus and the motivation to constantly seek improvement.

In April 2006 I received a leaflet from the Yorkshire Agricultural Society. The Best Chef in Yorkshire competition had started and the winner was to be crowned 'Professional Chef of the Year'. I looked at the leaflet pinned on our kitchen board everyday until I finally decided I just had to go for it. Apart from the glory of the title, the prize was a huge amount of free publicity and marketing which was the most valuable incentive. The entry requirement was to create and submit a recipe with strictly Yorkshire products. This was quite easy as using local products was something I had already been doing for several years and I had built good contacts with a lot of local farmers and producers. Weeks went by until I was notified that I was short listed from six hundred entries to be one of the final four.

The final stage was to be held at Harvey Nichols restaurant in Leeds and there was to be a cook off between the four chosen chefs each using the recipe they had submitted. The day of the final came fast, almost too fast. I had to take my daughter Nathalie to hospital that morning and the restaurant was full that night too. To add to the pressure I knew I had rehearsed the dish just once and I knew my timing wasn't good. Nonetheless, I was looking forward to the evening like a kid waiting for presents on Christmas morning.

Arriving early at Harvey Nichols, I was able to choose the best place in the kitchen and begin to focus on the task. We had ninety minutes to cook and present our dish. The judges on the night were considering methods, good practise, presentation, and of course flavours. I enjoyed every second of the contest and felt I couldn't have cooked better on the night. After forty five minutes of deliberation by the judges I was crowned 'Yorkshire Professional Chef of the Year' for 2006/07. This remains the greatest moment of my somewhat traumatic career. Something I could cherish forever, a far cry from that little boy back home with no real future. I was now Professional Chef of the Year!

This brought about a huge amount of publicity from across the region and from that moment on the restaurant was booked weeks in advance.

In the summer of 2008 having outgrown the small venue it had started in, Fennel relocated to much larger premises. In many ways it lost the very intimacy and personal character that had been instrumental to its success. After almost fourteen years in Wetherby with the onset of a severe economic down turn, Fennel had to shut down.

From Fennel to Mirabelle

The initial impact of the closure flattened my life almost like an earthquake. Friends, staff, business partners, my soul mate and my pride suddenly disappeared and I was left alone with nothing more than memories of happier times. The weeks following the closure of Fennel I was inundated with offers to take on restaurants across Yorkshire. Clearly the recession had taken its toll on the catering trade and so many premises, which had thrived during the economic boom of the last ten years, had switched off their lights too.

My confidence as a restaurateur had taken a severe bashing and my initial thought was to leave catering altogether. I almost automatically turned down the offers that came my way, but then a restaurant in the centre of Harrogate was brought to my attention. This was a small thirty six

seat restaurant situated on the ground floor of a four star hotel and the location was perfect. However, the thought of starting up again after a painful recent experience was just too much and I felt compelled to turn it down twice. Guy, the owner of the hotel had been my previous landlord and knew me well. Fortunately for me he refused to take no for an answer and eventually made me agree to just having a look. The seed was sown.

The place had been repossessed and was left in a poor state, however, the location was good and the deal on the table was financially solid. After visiting several times I began to think perhaps this might just work, and more importantly if I didn't give it a go, how would I ever know. I accepted the offer and the next few months were nothing short of a rollercoaster of emotions. After two financially disastrous years fighting for survival, my personal funds had run out. I hadn't kept up with my mortgage and my credit record was now beyond repair. To make matters worse my relationship of fifteen years had also collapsed under the immense pressure we were all under. Once again all I had was my passion for cooking. I basically had nothing more to lose, but somehow the passion was still holding out.

In order to earn some money the 2006 Yorkshire Professional Chef of the Year had to work for an agency cooking frozen burgers and chips. Sometimes humility is the only way to pay the bills. Every other waking moment was spent cleaning, decorating and preparing the new restaurant with the help of a small gang working for little more than another promise of good times to come.

Mirabelle opened its doors in December 2010. With the recession still very much affecting the economy and VAT being raised to twenty per cent, opening a restaurant was a risky thing to do. The two previous restaurant owners who had been in the premises before had gone bankrupt and the place did not have a good name for its dining experience. Yet I knew deep inside that the location was good and Harrogate is a large and affluent town so all I had to do was to find the winning formula I once had.

The first month was a financial disaster and once again I was running a restaurant at a loss. The pressure was on to somehow break the cycle. I had to remember I had made restaurants successful before and I had to convince myself this was going to work. In early January we began to attract local curiosity and Mirabelle managed to break even. Customers enjoyed our little restaurant and started telling friends. At the end of January the food Critic from the Yorkshire post wrote a review appreciating everything I was seeking to achieve. We have since become friends and I am delighted Elaine has written the foreword for this book.

For those who don't know, the Mirabelle plum tree is a native of Alsace. It produces small, smooth textured fruit that is sweet and full of flavour.

For those who haven't yet visited us, Mirabelle restaurant is a cosy little place to be found in Harrogate in the heart of Yorkshire. It is a smooth and refined environment offering food that is full of flavour and like the plum, aims to leave a sweet satisfying after taste.

When I consider the past and all the twists and turns I am very grateful and feel privileged to have achieved what I have achieved.

This book is a result of thirty years working in kitchens in France and England. From Alsace to Yorkshire a colourful and unique blend of two countries only separated by thirty three miles of water. Two countries so very different, but as far as food is concerned, we have found ways of sharing a common language. People often ask me if I would ever go back to Alsace and the answer is that I have found the best of both worlds.

A place in Alsace or a place in Yorkshire? - I simply wouldn't know how to choose between them.

Merci *beaucoup*

A big thanks...

I am of course indebted to a whole host of very talented chefs who, over the years, have shared their patience, experience, skill, techniques, and recipes.

A special thanks to all our customers past and present, without whom none of this incredible journey would have been possible, the strength of our restaurant lies in the loyalty of our staff past and present and to our suppliers who provide us with such great ingredients.

There are simply so many people I would like to thank but not enough space to name them all. Here are some of the special people who have impacted my life:

To my three wonderful children Jonathan, Nathalie and Alexander, I am forever grateful for the love, strength and support you have given me. The days where we worked together at Fig & Fennel will always remain some of the happiest days of my life.

Thanks to Johnnie Briggs for being there to pick up the pieces when I fell apart.

Thanks to Thomas Tiffon, your friendship and trust overwhelms me.

Thank you to Nic and Sally Sheppard, my Design and PR Gurus.

Thanks to Jon Goldsborough my dear friend and accountant.

Thanks to Rick and Sue Armstrong for being there when we needed you most.

Thanks to Oliver and Rachelle Leonard.

Thanks to Christine Harrison.

Thanks to Tom Jones, Martin 'Tinez' Freeman, Michael 'Jockey' Wilkinson, the Powell's, the McGill's and the Butterwick's!

And a very big thank you to Yvette Leonard and Gordon Harrison, I would not be where I am today without you.

A Trip to Alsace Lorraine

This short chapter is a trip down, memory lane but it's also a tribute to the people of Alsace Lorraine, an incredible will to survive torn by three wars with constant occupation the people fought to remain true to their French roots, with great traditions the people of Alsace Lorraine are proud of their terroir, crystal from Baccarat and Daum, our wines, our Mirabelle plums, our way of life and finally our food...

...I will pass on some of our recipes, deep rooted dishes that have remained authentic.

The originality of Alsace Lorrainelies in its diversity with a vast panorama of history, gastronomy, culture and museums. A broad spectrum of activities and natural beauty spots await you in this region of tradition, legends and unique festivals. Between the River Rhine and the Vosges mountains, through the plains, vineyards and mountains, along country lanes with fortresses and rich archaeological ruins on the horizon. Wander through the towns and villages with their startling architectural wealth combining typical rural styles and gems from the Mediaeval, Renaissance and Gothic periods....

Experience the wonders of a region which has carefully preserved its heritage. In Alsace, you will be greeted with a smile. The warm-hearted Alsatians with their living traditions and skilled craftwork inhabit a corner of France where the good life is a byword. Whether you go for the thrill of sports or the beauty of nature, you will find what you want, at the heart of the beauty you can stroll or hike... it's all here for the taking. Here you'll have all the time you need to experience life to the full. Local specialities, gourmet dishes, traditional flavour, vintage Alsace wines, beer and eau-de-vie... at the heart of a region where good living is an every day event.

Alsace wines are like no other French wines. The bottle shapes and grape varieties suggest a Germanic style, but the wines are drier and fuller than those from Germany with higher alcohol. A wide range of soils permits a wide range of grape varieties, making mostly rich or perfumed whites, with a single red variety. Alsace has a long growing season with warm dry autumns, allowing grapes to ripen reliably every vintage. In places, damp autumn mornings followed by hot days, give the right conditions too for excellent 'vendange tardive', dessert wines.

Lorraine is a spacious and wooded area with lakes, streams and rivers and acres of land left to grow wild mirabelle and prunes, you can sunbath on the side of the lakes in Gerardmer during the summer and ski in the winter, such is the diversity of Lorraine.

Food in Alsace Lorraine is heavily influence by its close border with Germany, historically this region was torn by occupation and war as it is the first to be occupied and the last to be freed.

We have become masters of smoked and cured meat, pickles and preserves, our fois gras is renowned across the world to be better than the Perigord.

Alsace Lorraine is now only one hour and forty minutes from Paris thanks to the TGV, this make Alsace Lorraine a must see region.

Mirabelle plums only grow in Lorraine this is the longest tarte aux mirabelles in the world (206.31 meters, or 4000 portions), Nancy, Place de la Carrière, 2 September 2006.

The mirabelle is a unique specialty of Lorraine, which has an ideal climate and soil composition for the cultivation of this fruit. This region produces fifteen thousand tons of mirabelle prunes annually, which constitutes 80% of global commercial production.

There are two main cultivars grown for fruit production, derived from cherry plums grown in Nancy and Metz. The Metz type is smaller, less hard, and less sweet, and has no small red spots on the skin. It is very good for jam, while the Nancy type is better as fresh fruit as it is sweeter.

Since 1996 the mirabelle de Lorraine has been recognized and promoted by the EU as a high-quality regional product, with a Protected Geographical Indication (PGI). This label guarantees a minimum fruit size and sugar content, and can only be used in a specific geographical zone of production.

The following are some favourite recipes from my beloved Lorraine

Crème de celeri au truffe des Vosges
Cream of celeriac with Vosges mountain truffles

Serves 4

800g celeriac
300g potatoes
50cl milk
50cl cream
50cl water
100g butter
20g whipped cream
10cl truffle oil or truffle juice
1 small truffle

1. Wash and peel the celeriac and the potatoes
2. Chop in small cubes
3. Place the butter in a large pan
4. Medium heat
5. Add the vegetables
6. Stir gently until the vegetables are coated with butter without browning
7. Add the water, milk, cream and truffle oil
8. Cook for 40 minutes
9. Blend the soup well
10. Taste for seasoning
11. Add salt and pepper if needed
12. Serve with a dollop of whip cream and slice of truffle

Salad Vosgienne
Warm Salad

Serves 4

3 endive or chicory lettuce

150g of smoked bacon

4 eggs

100g of croutons

4tbs white wine vinegar

10cl cream

Rapeseed oil

Salt and pepper

20g butter

1. Wash and prepare the lettuce
2. Melt the butter and olive oil in a frying pan
3. Fry the bacon well
4. Remove the bacon carefully
5. Deglaze the frying pan with the vinegar
6. Add the cream then reduce gently
7. Add salt and pepper if needed
8. In a pan of boiling water with a little vinegar poach the eggs for 3 minutes
9. Retrieve carefully and set aside
10. Place the lettuce in the centre of the plate
11. Add the bacon, The croutons and the egg
12. Pour the reduction over the top
13. Serve immediately

Quiche au Munster and cumin
Munster cheese and cumin quiche

Serves 4

250g short crust pastry

150 Munster

1 egg

1 egg yolk

15cl cream

10cl milk

Salt and pepper

1 teaspoon of cumin

1. Line your mould with the pastry
2. Dice the Munster and spread equally in the lined quiche mould
3. Mix in a medium bowl 1 egg, 1 egg yolk, cream, milk, salt and pepper
4. Add the cumin
5. Pour the mixture into the lined mould
6. Cook for 30 minutes at 180*C
7. Serve with a mixed leaf salad

Cake au jambon
Savoury ham cake
Serves 8

240g plain flour

1tbs of baking powder

4 eggs

8tbs of milk

150g of grated gruyere

Salt and pepper

70g of smoked bacon

100g roast ham

1. Dice the bacon and ham
2. Pan Fry the bacon and ham without any fat (the bacon will have sufficient fat to cook)
3. In a large bowl add the flour, baking powder, eggs, milk, grated cheese, the ham and bacon
4. Mix well
5. Place the mixture in an 8 inch oven dish lined with greaseproof paper
6. Cook for 40 to 50 minutes
7. Best served cold

Ma quiche Lorraine!
Served worldwide with millions of different recipes but this is the one and only original recipe… we don't put cheese in it!

Serves 4

200g smoke streaky bacon

200g crème fraiche

4 eggs

Salt and pepper

Nutmeg

250g short crust pastry

1. Cut the streaky bacon in chunks
2. In a frying pan pour the bacon without fat
3. Cook on a high heat for 5 minutes
4. In a mixing bowl add the eggs, cream, grated nutmeg, salt and pepper
5. Line a mould with the pastry
6. Add the bacon
7. Then pour in the mixture
8. Cook for 20 minutes at 180*C

Poire au vin rouge
Poached pears in red wine
Serves 4-6

1kg pear

1 bottle of red wine

150 sugar

1 vannila pod

1 lemon

1 orange

2 cinamon sticks

10cl crème de cassis

1. Peel the pears
2. Cut into 4
3. Remove the core
4. In a pan, pour the wine
5. Bring to the boil
6. Set it alight to remove the alcohol
7. Add the cinnamon sticks, vanilla pod, crème de cassis, lemon and orange and sugar
8. Bring to the boil for 5 minutes
9. Add the pears
10. Cook for 15 minutes and leave to cool overnight
11. Serve hot or cold

Gateaux aux-myrtilles
Bilberry sponge cake
Serves 4

75g natural yogurt

150g sugar

100g self-raising flour

100g double cream

4 eggs

200g bilberries

1. In a mixing bowl place the yogurt, cream, eggs, flour, sugar and the bilberries
2. Mix until smooth
3. Place in a sponge cake mould
4. Cook for 40 minutes at 180°C
5. Serve hot or cold

Jams and chutneys
My Mum's Jams!

Jam making is easy and so rewarding. This chapter shows you how to create great homemade jams, marmalade and chutneys that are so much better than those you buy in supermarkets.

You should always make jam when the fruit you are using are in season, they are so much better and cheaper too.

I will explain how to choose and prepare the fruit, what equipment to use, how to test when setting point is reached. I will also explain the importance of natural pectin and acid in the fruits these recipes have been tried and tested in our restaurant kitchen. It is very satisfying to eat something you have made yourself and a jar of homemade jam, marmalade or chutney makes a thoughtful gift for friends and family.

For some of my recipes I suggest using sugar with added pectin. As you will see in the list below some fruits are low in natural pectin and for a successful outcome you may need to use sugar with added natural pectin.

Fruit high in pectin
Cooking apple
Crab apple
Black and red currant
Gooseberries
Grapes and plums
Quinces
Lemons and limes

Fruit low in pectin
Apricots
Peaches
Cherries
Raspberries
Strawberries
Pineapple
Melon
Pears

My mum's jams!

Setting Point

The setting point is the exact time to finish cooking the jam or marmalade, the jam will not set properly if it does not reach it, and if the cooking goes beyond this point the jam will crystallise.

After trying several methods the best one by far is as my mum would call it 'the saucers method'.

When you are just about to start the jam or marmalade take two saucers and place them in the freezer. When you think the jam has reach setting point take one saucer out and drop a spoonful of jam onto it, place it back in the freezer for thirty seconds.

Take it out, it should crinkle if you push it with your finger, turn the plate upside down if the jam still sticks, the setting point is reached.

Chutneys

The original chutney was first made in India and was usually a relish made from fresh fruits and spices. During the colonial era the British took the recipe back to Britain, the recipe has changed a little since then and it is now served with cold meat, pates and terrine but also with roast pork and venison.

Cooked with mango, papaya or apple, chutneys are common in the Caribbean, and chutneys are also widely used in South Africa. They have become increasingly popular in the U.S., especially with the rise in popularity of Caribbean curries.

Chutneys are served with almost every meal in India. They can be fresh or cooked, and are made from a wide variety of ingredients. They range in flavour from sweet or sour, spicy or mild, or any combination of these; they can be thin or chunky and can be made with fruits or vegetables or both. Mangos, apples, pears, tamarind, onions, lemon, tomato, raisins, coconut, vinegar, sugar, honey, citrus peel, garlic, ginger, mint, turmeric, cinnamon, and hot chilies are some of the ingredients used.

Confiture de figues
Fig jam

This jam has a lovely colour and a sticky texture. You can also use this jam as a base for some great desserts for example, pour over poached pear or mix with whipped cream, crème de cassis and crushed meringue and put into a wine glass then finish with fresh raspberries.

1kg fresh figs
1 lemon
250ml water
500g sugar

1. Wash and take the stalks off the figs
2. Peel the lemon and cut the peel into thin strips and juice the lemon
3. Add it to the jam pan together with the figs and the water
4. Slowly bring to the boil stirring frequently until the figs are soft
5. Add sugar and stir until dissolved
6. Boil a little faster until you reach setting point

    Please refer to the first page of this chapter for setting point

Confiture de peches et fruit de la passion
Peach and passion fruit jam

Passion fruit goes very well with peach. The sweetness of the peach and the tartness of the passion fruit work wonders. You can also use the jam as a base for many tropical desserts.

Make this jam at the height of the peach season they are much better and cheaper too.

10 passion fruits
2kg peaches, ripe if possible
Juice and zest of 2 lemons
2kg granulated sugar with added pectin

1. Extract the pulp from the passion fruit
2. Take the skin off the peaches - simply keep the peaches in boiling water for 3 minutes
3. Roughly cut the peaches into small pieces and place in a saucepan together with the sugar, lemon juice, zest and passion fruit, slowly bring to the boil then boil rapidly until setting point is reached
4. Remove from the heat
5. Leave to cool before storing in jars

Confiture d'ananas et rubarbe
Rhubarb and pineapple jam

This is a tasty breakfast jam, the addition of the pineapple brings a touch of tropical flavour. Use a very ripe pineapple if possible.

1 medium size pineapple
1kg chopped rhubarb
1kg sugar
Juice and rind of 2 oranges

1. Wash the rhubarb and cut into pieces
2. Put into a large saucepan
3. Sprinkle with the sugar, orange juice and peel
4. Mix with a wooden spoon and leave for 1 hour
5. Chop the pineapple into small cubes
6. Put the pineapple in the jam pan and stir in
7. Bring to the boil and cook slowly for 30 minutes, stirring often
8. Check setting point
9. Allow the jam to cool for 1 hour before putting into sterilised jars

Confiture de fraises
Strawberry jam

The best jam in the world, strawberries must have been created for jam!

If you wait until the fruit are in season, picking your own strawberries from the farm rather than buy from supermarkets, they are cheaper and taste so much better,

Make a few batches during the season and you can enjoy strawberry jam during the winter months.

2kg granulated sugar
2kg fresh strawberries
Juice and zest of 2 lemons

1. Put the strawberries in the jam pan
2. Add the lemon juice and peel
3. Heat gently, stirring as the juice begins to flow out of the fruit
4. When the juice is coming to the boil, add the sugar
5. Stir well until dissolved, bring the jam rapidly to the boil until it thickens, approx., 15 to 20 minutes or until it reaches setting point
6. Remove from the heat and leave to cool for 30 minutes before putting into jars

Pates de fruits
Fruit jelly

A good fruit jelly is usually bright, clear, set but still wobbly.

The same basic rules that apply the jam apply here. The only difference is you are straining the juice from cooked fruit, discard the fruit and mix the juice with the sugar until reaching setting point.

Gelee de pommes
Apple jelly

For best results we use windfall apple or crab apple for this recipe. Great with roast pork, toasted goats cheese, wild boar or simply on toast.

2kg of apples or crab apples
Granulated sugar

1. Peel, core and chop the apples and put them in a jam pan
2. Pour on enough water to just cover the fruit
3. Cook for 1 hour
4. Strain the mixture through a jelly bag hanging over a large bowl
   This is a slow process but necessary
5. Try not to disturb the straining as the juice may become cloudy
6. Measure the juice, then add 250gr of sugar for every 250 ml of fruit juice
7. Bring to the boil until it reaches setting point
8. Remove from the heat
9. Skim off the foam made by the sugar
10. Pour into sterilised jars straight away

Gelee de coings
Quince jelly

Quince is an underrated fruit when it comes to making jelly. It has a lovely light red colour, great with pork or lamb, widely used in Spain with cheese, the flavour is delicate, sweet and subtle.

1kg quinces
1.5 litre water
Granulated sugar - *250g of sugar for every 250ml of juice*

1. Clean the quinces well, removing the fur that covers the fruit
2. Cut into small cubes
3. Place the fruit into a large saucepan
4. Pour the water onto the fruit and bring to the boil
5. Simmer until the fruit is soft
6. Strain the juice through a jelly bag into a clean saucepan, this is a slow process, leave it to drain overnight if you can
7. Do not disturb the juice too much
8. Bring the juice to the boil and add the sugar slowly, stir in until the sugar has dissolved
9. Bring to the boil until setting point is reached

Note: use crab apple or red currant instead of the quinces following the same method.

Marmalade

Pink grapefruit marmalade is a brilliant breakfast jam much better when thick.

Try to pick the grapefruit slightly under ripe for a better marmalade.

3 large pink grapefruits
1 lemon
1.2kg sugar high in pectin
1.5 litre of water

1. Cut the grapefruit and the lemon in half
2. Squeeze out the juice
3. Pour into a large saucepan
4. Cut the skin into strips - usually 2 grapefruit is enough it make a better marmalade
5. Place the skins into the saucepan with the juice
6. Bring to the boil
7. Simmer for 45 minutes
8. Add the sugar and stir until dissolved
9. Bring to the boil until setting point is reached
10. Leave to rest for 30 minutes then it's ready to jar

Marmalade a l'ancienne
Old fashioned marmalade

I know that marmalade is widely available in shops and supermarket but it will never be as good as the one you make yourself. This is a 1 hour recipe but the result is brilliant.

It is better to use Seville oranges for marmalade however they are not available all year round. Usually you can only get Seville around Christmas until late February. We use any good quality oranges for this recipe. You can also use blood oranges if you are lucky enough to find any.

If you plan ahead, like most jams and marmalade, make these during the peak of the season they usually are better quality and again often cheaper too. This recipe makes a dozen jars enough to last you a year!

2kg of oranges
1 lemon juice
4 litre of water
4kg of high in pectin sugar

1. Cut the orange in half then squeeze out the juice
2. Cut all the peel into strips according to your liking, thin or thick cut
3. Pour the juice of the lemon and orange into a large saucepan together with the peel
4. Bring slowly to the boil then simmer fast for one hour
5. Add the sugar, stir until dissolved
6. Bring to the boil for 15 minutes until setting point is reached
7. Leave to cool before storing in jars

Chutney de Poire aux epices
Spicy pear chutney

4 ripe pears
1 bramley apple
100g sultanas
2 small red chillies
1 large onion
150g brown sugar
150ml of malt vinegar
1 teaspoon of Chinese 5 spices

1. Peel and cut the pears the apple, onion into cubes
2. Put into a large saucepan
3. Add the sugar, vinegar and sultanas
4. Cut the chillies into small cubes
5. Add to the mixture
6. Cook slowly for 45 minutes stirring frequently
7. Leave to cool for 2 hours before pouring into jars
8. For best results the chutney should rest for at least 2 weeks before use

Chutney de Airelle
Cranberry chutney

Ideal for pork and of course turkey. I developed this recipe for Christmas. Fresh cranberries are in season from November but you can also use a jar of cranberry sauce.

250g of fresh cranberry or 1 jar of Cranberry Sauce
50g raisins
1 diced apple
100g granulated sugar
100ml malt vinegar
Half tsp ground allspice
Half tsp ground ginger
Half ground cinnamon
Dash ground cloves

1. Combine all ingredients in a medium saucepan
2. Cook on medium heat, stirring occasionally, until apples are tender and sauce has thickened slightly, about 30 minutes
3. Leave to cool and store in jars

Nos pains
Bread

There is nothing more satisfying than biting into the crisp crust and crumbly inside of a homemade bread roll not to mention the aroma. Making bread is a pleasure too as you can work off the day's frustrations during the kneading process! The range of bread in supermarkets is on the increase and it seems as if there is little point in home baking but the arrival of the bread machine has made bread making much more accessible to everyone.

I am not a great fan of machines when it comes to bread, it does not take a great deal more time to make it by hand, first you can choose the shape, with the machine you can't and the taste of the bread is far better. However it is certainly worth making bread for special occasions or making an everyday meal a bit of a treat.

Ingredients are important. Fresh yeast is much better than dried and if possible use organic flour. Most supermarkets and specialist retailers have it and here at Mirabelle we are always glad to give you some.

The basic recipe remains the same throughout all my bread making and the method stays the same too, this will help you achieve great results all the time whether you are making a plain brown loaf or focaccia.

Here are a few simple rules

1. Light your oven as bread needs heat to prove
2. Use lukewarm water to melt your yeast
3. Knead the dough for at least 5 minutes to produce a light texture loaf
4. Do not leave the dough in a draught to prove
5. Cover the dough while proving
6. All my recipes make 4 loaves of 400gr.
7. The bread freezes extremely well so why not make enough for your next dinner party

Techniques

Using fresh yeast

Crumble fresh yeast into a measuring jug, add a pinch of sugar, pour the water or milk onto the yeast, the liquid must be warm (not hot) to accelerate the proving process, stir it until the yeast is totally melted. Prove the dough once in a bowl then once again after shaping.

Adding fat

Diced butter may be added to the dry ingredients. Rub the fat between your fingers until the mixture resembles breadcrumbs. Using olive oil is much better and healthier too, just add it with the liquid.

Kneading the dough

To ensure a good rise knead the dough thoroughly for at least 5 minutes on a lightly flour surface. Fold the dough towards you, then push it away from you with the heel of your hand, turn the dough, repeat the action until the dough is smooth and elastic.

Proving

Proving means leaving the dough aside to rise. Dough made with dried yeast only needs to be proved once. With fresh yeast the dough need to prove once in the bowl and once again after shaping, proving time vary according to the temperature of you kitchen often lighting your oven at a low heat before starting the bread help proving, often better to leave the dough covered with a cloth or cling film on top of the stove for 20 minutes or until it double in size.

Baking

Cooking will vary depending on the size of the bread and a preheated oven 200*c/400*f/gas mark 6 should be sufficient. Glaze the bread with milk for a golden finish and bake for 25 to 30 minutes. Allow to cool on a wire rack.

Testing bread

At the end of the cooking time, hold the loaf upside down and tap it gently on the base, if it sounds hollow, the bread is ready.

Pain aux nois et beteraves
Walnut and beetroot loaf
Makes 4 loaves

This is a brilliant bread to serve with meaty starters such as pate and terrine, the blend of walnut and beetroot works well and the colour is great. These are some of the funky breads we make at the restaurant, it's a basic brown bread with a few extras.

400g strong white flour
400g strong brown flour
150g wholemeal flour
100g chopped walnuts
1 grated raw beetroot
1tsp sugar
1tsp salt
600ml warm water
40g fresh yeast

1. Preheat the oven to 220°/gas7
2. Put the flour, salt, sugar, walnut into a large bowl
3. Melt the fresh yeast to the warm water
4. Pour the mixture into the flour and mix to a soft dough
5. Knead for at least 10 minutes
6. Leave to prove for about 15 minutes
9. Knock the dough back to its original size and shape into a bowl
10. Leave to prove for 30 minutes glaze gently
11. Bake for 30 minutes or until dark brown

Citrouille et pistaches
Butternut squash and pistachio
Makes 4 loaves or 16 rolls

A variation of flavours and colours make this bread a great dinner party roll or loaf, great for starters but also useful for soups too.

600g strong white flour
400g gr strong brown flour
100g chopped ready salted pistachios
100g of grated raw butternut squash
2tbs honey
1tsp sugar
1tsp salt
600ml warm water
40g fresh yeast

1. Preheat the oven to 220°/gas7
2. Put the flour, salt, sugar, pistachio, butternut squash into a large bowl
3. Melt the fresh yeast to the warm water add the honey
4. Pour the mixture into the flour and mix to a soft dough
5. Knead for at least 10 minutes
6. Leave to prove for about 30 minutes
9. Knock the dough back to its original size and shape into a bowl
10. Leave to prove for 30 minutes glaze gently
11. Bake for 35 minutes or until dark brown

Tomate et basilique
Sundried tomato and basil loaf
Makes 4 loaves or 16 rolls

No Italian meal is ever served without bread like this one, this one comes from Tuscany where the tomatoes are really sun dried.

1 kg of strong flour preferably type 00
50g sundried tomatoes finely chopped
300ml milk
300ml water
30g fresh yeast
2 tsp salt
1 tsp sugar
1 tbs of red pesto of fresh basil
1 beaten egg for glazing

1. Preheat the oven to 220°C gas mark 7
2. Sieve flour into a large bowl
3. Add the salt, sugar, pesto and sun dried tomatoes mix well
4. Warm gently the milk and water 37*C add the yeast and stir until melted
5. Pour the mixture into the flour
6. Mix to a soft dough
7. Knead for 5 minutes
8. Leave to prove for about 15 minutes
9. Knock the dough back to it's original size and shape into a small loaf or baguette
10. Leave to prove for 30 minutes glaze gently
11. Bake for 30 minutes or until golden brown

Parmesan et poivrons rouge
Pollenta, parmesan and red pepper

Makes 4 loaves

Full of Mediterranean flavour, this bread is best eaten warm or toasted drizzled with olive oil.

700g strong white flour

300g polenta

1 red pepper

50g fresh parmesan shavings

2 tsp salt

2 tsp sugar

35g fresh yeast

500ml warm water

1. Preheat the oven to 220°C gas mark 7
2. Slice thinly the red pepper and gently stir fry in olive oil
3. Put the flour, polenta, parmesan, salt and sugar in a large bowl
4. Add the red pepper
5. Melt the fresh yeast in warm water then pour it into the mixture
6. Mix to a soft dough
7. Knead for at least 5 minute
8. Leave to prove for about 15 minutes
9. Knock the dough back to it's original size and put it in a medium size loaf tin
10. Leave to prove for 30 minutes glaze gently
11. Bake for 30 minutes or until pale gold

Pain aux noix
Walnut cob
Make 4 loaves

This traditional Alsace loaf, made from a mixture of wholemeal and stoneground brown flour, perfect with cheese and a glass of Riesling of course!

800g strong brown flour

150g wholemeal flour

100g chopped walnuts

1tsp sugar

1tsp salt

1tsp honey

300ml warm water

300ml warm milk

40g fresh yeast

1. Preheat the oven to 220°/gas7.
2. Put the flour, salt, sugar, walnut into a large bowl
3. Melt the fresh yeast to the warm milk and water
4. Pour the mixture into the flour and mix to a soft dough
5. Knead for at least 10 minutes
6. Leave to prove for about 15 minutes
7. Knock the dough back to it's original size and shape into a bowl
8. Leave to prove for 30 minutes glaze gently
9. Bake for 30 minutes or until dark brown

Tomate et ognions rouge avec romarin
Tomato, red onion and rosemary focaccia

Makes 5 focaccia

Now in fashion in all top restaurants this Italian bread is enriched with olive oil, ideal with antipasto or soup.

1kg strong white flour preferably type 45

3tbs olive oil

1tps sugar

2tps salt

600ml warm water

40g yeast

1 large red onion roughly chopped

4 tomatoes roughly cut

Fresh rosemary

Rock salt

1. Put the flour, salt and sugar into a large bowl
2. In a measuring jug add the yeast with the olive oil and the warm water, stir until melted
3. Pour into the flour and mix to a soft dough
4. Knead for 5 minutes
5. Leave to prove for 15 minutes
6. Knock back to original size, divide the dough into 5 balls, then using a rolling pin roll the dough into a round shape making sure you leave quite thick
7. Using your finger, dimple the dough all over, brush it to the edge with olive oil and sprinkle with rock salt
8. Put the onion, tomato and rosemary onto the foccacia
9. Leave to prove for 20 minutes
10. Bake for 20 minutes or until dark brown

Pain au raisins sec et noisettes
Hazelnut and raisin loaf

Make 4 loaves

I picked up this recipe from Scandinavian where this bread is very popular, try with cheese or simply with jam for breakfast.

550g of organic brown flour

250g of wholemeal flour

200g strong white flour

2 tbs of clear honey

1 tsp of salt

115g of organic raisin

50g of chopped walnuts

500 ml of fresh milk

50g of fresh yeast

1. Sieve all the flour into a bowl, stir in the salt, sultanas and walnuts
2. Melt the yeast in the warm milk and make a well in the centre of the dry ingredients pour onto the flour
3. Mix to a soft dough and knead for at least 5 minutes
4. Leave to prove until double the size
5. Knock back to its original size and shape into a long sausage
6. Make about 4 cut diagonal cuts and glaze with milk
7. Leave to prove for a further 20 minutes
8. Bake in a preheated oven 220°C/gas 6/7 for 20 to 25 minutes

Pain de seigle
Rye bread

Make 4 loaves

Originally from Germany this bread has become one of our best-selling recipes, great with seafood or smoked fish.

500g of strong organic brown flour
300g strong organic rye flour
200g strong organic white flour
2 tsp of salt
60g fresh yeast
50g rye flakes (optional)
2 tsp caraway seed optional
500 ml water

1.   Sieve the flour together into a large bowl
2.   Add salt, rye flakes and caraway seeds
3.   Melt the yeast in the measuring jug then pour onto the dry mixture
4.   Mix to a soft dough and knead for at least 5 minutes
5.   Leave to prove until double the size
6.   Knock back to its original size and shape into a long oval loaf
7.   Make about 4 diagonal cuts across the top and glaze with milk
8.   Leave to prove for a further 20 minutes and bake to a preheated oven 220°C/gas 6/7 for 20 to 25 minutes

Fromage et oignons
Cheese and onion loaf

Make 4 loaves

1kg strong organic white flour

100g sliced onion

50g mature cheddar diced into small cubes

2 tbs olive oil

2 tsp salt

pinch of black pepper

pinch of sugar

50g fresh yeast

500 ml water

1 tsp cumin

1. Peel and slice onion and cook gently with olive oil, add salt and pepper and a pinch of sugar this will help caramelised the onion, cook for 15 minutes very slowly.
2. Mix the flour with salt, diced cheese, onion and cumin
3. Melt the yeast with warm water pour onto the dry mixture
4. Mix to a soft dough and knead for at least 5 minutes
5. Leave to prove until double the size
6. Knock back to its original size and shape into a round bowl
7. Make about 4 cut diagonal cuts and glaze with milk
8. Leave to prove for a further 20 minutes and bake to a preheated oven 220°C/gas 6/7 for about 20 to 25 minutes

Ciabatta aux olives
Ciabatta roll with olives
Makes 3 loaves

This irregular shape Italian bread is made with a very wet dough and flavoured with olive oil.

40g of fresh yeast
400ml of warm water
60ml warm milk
500g unbleached white bread flour
2 tsp salt
3tbs extra olive oil
50g pitted olives
For the starter:
10g fresh yeast
200ml warm water
350g unbleached bread flour

1. Melt the yeast for the starter in the warm water
2. Gradually mix the yeast mixture and the flour to form a firm dough
3. Turn out the starter dough onto a lightly floured surface and knead for 5 minutes
4. Leave to prove for around 12 hours - you can prepare this the day before.
5. Melt the yeast for the dough with the warmed water, add in the starter and gradually mix
6. Add the warm milk, the rest of the flour with the chopped olives using a wooden spoon. This will take a few minutes and will form a very wet dough impossible to knead on a work surface, beat in the salt and olive oil
7. Cover and prove for 30 minute or double size
8. Using a spoon carefully tip a third of the dough onto a lightly floured baking tray
9. Roll into a rough loaf shape, sprinkle with flour and leave for 30 minutes
10. Place in a preheated oven at 220°C/ gas 7 and bake for 25 minutes

Pain a l'ail
Garlic loaf
Makes 4 loaves

Unsual, different,and sexy!

1kg strong white flour
4 garlic gloves
  more if you really like garlic
2 tsp salt
1 pinch of black pepper
A large bunch of fresh parsley
2 tsp olive oil
50g fresh yeast

1. Peel and slice the garlic and gently fried until crisp leave to cool
2. Chopped the parsley and add to the garlic mixture
3. Put the flour, salt, pepper and the garlic mixture in a large bowl
4. Melt the yeast in a measuring jug with warm water pour into the dry mixture mix to a dough
5. Knead for at least 5 minutes
6. Leave to prove for 20 to 30 minutes then knock back to original size then shape into a loaf tin
7. Prove again until double the size then bake in a preheated oven at 200°C/ gas 6 for 25 to 30 minutes

Brioche

Makes 1 loaf

Rich, buttery, yet its light, brilliant for breakfast, the best bread in France.

350g unbleached white bread flour
☐ tsp salt
25g fresh yeast
60ml warm milk
3 large eggs
175g unsalted butter
25g caster sugar
For the glazing:
1 egg yolk
1 tsp milk

1. Sieve the flour into a large bowl, melt the yeast in the warm milk, then pour into the flour, add the eggs and mix to a soft dough
2. Beat the dough for 3 to 5 minutes, cream the butter and sugar together
3. Gradually add the butter to the dough in small amount
4. Beat until smooth and elastic and leave to prove for an hour
5. Lightly knock back the dough and place in the fridge for an hour
6. Shape the brioche in a loaf tin or a brioche mould if you have
7. Glaze the brioche with the egg yolk and milk mixture cover and leave for at lest 1 hour or double the size
8. Preheat the oven to 230°C/ gas 8, put the brioche in the oven then turn the temp to 190°C/ gas 5 and bake for 25 to 30 minutes
9. Turn out on to a rack and leave to cool

Nos Entrees
Starters

A successful dinner party starts with a well chosen starter, although there are very few guidelines as to what you should cook for a dinner party here are a few rules you must try to keep, fish starter, meat main course or vice versa.

Complicated and heavy main courses require a light starter.

Try to follow the seasons when you pick your ingredients, as when in season fruits, vegetables, meat and fish often cost less and are fuller in flavour.

Remember the starter should only be small and well presented as you have a full meal ahead.

Here are ten of my favourite starters:

Level of difficulty:
Level 1 simple
Level 2 easy and fast
Level 3 difficult but worth it
Level 4 hard but impressive finishes

Note:
All spoon measures are level or as otherwise stated
1tsp = 5ml
1tbs = 15ml
Eggs used in the recipes are free-range medium unless stated
Oven time:
All recipes unless stated are for fan assisted ovens
For conventional oven add 20°C

The timings provided are just guidelines and you must rely on your own judgement as to when a dish is properly cooked as there is a huge difference in cooking times between say an Aga and a powerful fan assisted oven.

Stocks and sauces:
There are now plenty of stocks and sauces available in good supermarkets and specialist retailers and in all forms, tinned, cartons, fresh, dried or cubed.

Each recipe in this book will state the best one to use.

Herbs used in these recipes are fresh.

Pate en croute a l'Anglaise
Posh pie and peas, port sauce

Level 4   Serves 6

Posh pie and peas was invented on a Sunday in December when Barry the butcher kindly asked me to help him bone turkeys in the back of his butcher shop.

Whilst getting on with the mind numbing job, on the other side of the shop the butcher was making pork pies and I started thinking of what else could you put in a pork pie pastry? So I came up with a small pie filled with duck confit, foie gras and truffle, a flavoursome combination.

Tips: save small tins of baked beans from the supermarket cut open both sides make sure you have removed tops and bottoms safely smoothing out all inner sides

Filling:
2 duck legs
100g of foie gras - optional
2 garlic gloves
1 small onion
Olive oil or goose fat
Flat parsley
Mushy peas see recipe page

Pastry:
400g plain flour
200g lard
salt
water

Prepare the duck:

1. Place the duck legs in the oven for 1 hour at 180°C
2. Leave to cool
3. Keep the remaining fat and juices from the roasting tin as you will need it later
4. If you have goose fat, please see duck confit recipe page

Prepare the pastry:

1. In a blender put the flour, lard, salt and water
2. Blend until all ingredients form a ball
3. Leave to rest for 20 minutes
4. Take the meat off the bone then cut into small cubes
5. Finely chop the onion and garlic, pour it into the roasting tin, cook gently for 5 minutes, add the duck and cook for a further 5 minutes season to taste
6. Remove the duck and prepare the port sauce
7. Pour a glass of port in the roasting tin, add 2 tbs of gravy granules, 2 glasses of water
8. Reduce to the equivalent of 3 tbs per pies then add a 25g of butter
9. Season to taste

Prepare the moulds:

1. Roll a third of the pastry, use the moulds to cut 6 tops
2. Roll the remaining pastry then gently line the moulds cutting with a scissors the excess of pasty
3. Fill the moulds with the mixture
4. Fold the pastry over, brush with egg yolk to seal the pastry, cover with the cut pastry tops
5. Brush with the remaining egg yolk
6. Bake for 30 minutes at 165°C

Timbale de fromage a la rubarbe, gelee de pommes pain aux noix

Tian of Mrs Bell's Olde Yorke with crab apple, rhubarb wrapped with oak smoked venison with organic walnut toast

Serve 6   Level 3

The wining dish

This recipe was developed in April 2006. I had just received an entry form for the Yorkshire Chef of the year award to be held later that year, I went on to win the award with this recipe.

Ingredients:

500g of Mrs Bell's Olde Yorke (can be substituted with crumbly goats cheese or Wensleydale)

100g crab apple

100g red rhubarb

250g of thinly slice smoked venison (can be substituted with Parma Ham)

Salt and pepper

Crab apple jelly:

See jam and chutney chapter for recipe

Walnut bread:

See bread chapter for recipe

Method:

1. Place the cheese in a medium size bowl
2. Using a potato masher or fork, reduce the cheese to crumbs
3. Peel and cut the the rhubarb and apples into small cubes and place In a small sauce pan
4. Sweat fruit with a little butter for 5 minutes without browning
5. Add the cooked fruits to the cheese
6. Season to taste
7. Stir until smooth
8. Divide into 6 medium size moulds 3"

    Make sure you carry this out on the plate you will serve the dish
9. With the back of a spoon push the mixture into a flat, well-rounded shape
10. Remove carefully from the mould
11. Wrap the smoked venison around the cheese
12. Place a little frisee lettuce on top of the cheese
13. Serve with a spoon of crab apple jelly, toasted walnut bread and unsalted butter

Rillette de crab, salad d'avocat, pain de seigle
Whitby crab rillette, avocado salad, toasted rye bread

Serves 6   Level 1

Whitby trawlers bring some of the finest crab into Britain, the flavour is sweet and the texture is soft, it's only by supporting our local fisherman that we can keep our coast alive. Next time you are at the seaside purchase some crab wrap, it well and freeze it for next time you have a dinner party and you can do this simple yet flavoursome recipe.

3 fresh dressed crab

3 tbs seafood sauce or cocktail sauce

Half cucumber

Fresh chives

Flat parsley

Salt and pepper

1 ripe avocado

1 red pepper

Olive oil

Organic rye loaf - See bread chapter

Method:

If you have fresh crab:

1. Pour 1 litre of salted water into a pan
2. Cook the crab for 10 minutes on a low temperature
3. Turn off the gas and leave for a further 10 minutes
4. Remove from the pan and leave to cool

Preparing the dish:

1. Pour the flesh into a medium size bowl, ensure no pieces of shell are left in the flesh
2. Add chopped chives and parsley
3. Season with salt and pepper
4. Add the cocktail sauce
5. Mix into a smooth paste
6. Divide into 6 small size moulds
7. Slice cucumber thinly and place around the crab
8. Cut the avocado and the red pepper in cubes and place around the crab rillette
9. Sprinkle with olive oil

Salad tiede do boudin et lard fume

Warm salad of Yorkshire bacon and black pudding, topped with a poached egg

Serves 4 Level 1

This recipe is a testimony to James Wright butcher in Ingleby North Yorkshire
3 generations of Yorkshire butchers, he once brought a sample of his bacon to the restaurant, the bacon is cured the old fashion way and without any unnecessary chemical or flavour enhancers.

Since having a restaurant I have come to realise how fortunate we are to have such passionate and skilled butchers ,fishermen, and of course farmers within 40 miles of our restaurant.
The success of this recipe depends on the quality of your bacon and black pudding
Easy recipe to prepare with a great finish

6 dry cured rashes of good bacon

8 small piece of black pudding

A nice mixture of lettuce, rocket and frizee

Walnut oil

Balsamic vinegar

Salt/ pepper

4 free range eggs

2 tbs of malt vinegar

1. Wash and chop roughly the lettuce
2. Place the lettuce in the center of the plate
3. Add salt, pepper, olive oil and balsamic vinegar
4. Cut the bacon into small cubes
5. Place the bacon in a non stick frying pan with the black pudding
6. Pan-fried with a tbs of olive oil until very crispy
7. Bring to the boil 500 ml of water with a tbs of malt vinegar (the vinegar will coagulate the egg white)
8. Break the egg into a cup and add to the boiling water
9. Cook for 2 minutes
10. Place equal amounts of bacon and black pudding onto the lettuce
11. Pour on the warm olive oil
12. With a straining spoon retrieve the egg from the water and drain
13. Gently place the egg on top of the lettuce
14. Finish with a drizzle of olive oil

Beignets de crab a la Thailandaise
Thai fish cakes coriander and sweet chilli and coriander relish

Serves 4   Level 1

A brilliant starter from Thailand to which we added a little Yorkshire! Thanks to Fred Martin who gave me the recipe. Fred was a miner all his life until becoming a pub landlord with a passion as big as mine for food. Thanks Fred!! Such an easy, light and flavoursome starter, you can make it as hot or mild as you like. It can be prepared the day before.

300g of salmon or haddock
1 or 2 tbs of Thai red curry paste
1 tbs of fish sauce
1 egg
20g freshly chopped coriander
1 stick of lemon grass finely chopped
2 finely chopped spring onion
Vegetable oil
Sweet chilli sauce

1. Pour all the ingredients into a blender blend for a 1 to 2 minutes
2. Leave to rest in the fridge for 30 minutes
3. Pour 100ml of vegetable oil into a non-stick frying pan
4. The oil must be warm but not hot
5. Shape the mixture into 8 round cakes
6. Place gently into the frying pan
7. Cook for 3 minutes then turn the fish cake over
8. Finish in the oven for 10 minutes

Moules marinieres ma facon
My moules mariniere
Serves 4

Moules mariniere has many different variations according to the region, in Brittany they use just white wine, in Normandy they add cream and in the south they add tomatoes. Whatever way you choose to make it, they will be full of flavour, first you must choose the mussels.

Most fish mongers and fish counters in supermarkets sell mussels. There are plenty of theories as to when the mussels are at their best, but the truth is nowadays the mussels are farmed throughout the year.

Rope mussels are the best as they never touch the bottom of the sea, this is good as they do not contain sand and are possibly cleaner.

Scottish mussels are popular as are those from France.

2kg fresh mussels
50g chopped shallots
3 garlic gloves crushed
Handful chopped flat leaves parsley
50g chopped onion
2tbs olive oil
20g unsalted butter
250ml white wine
150ml double cream
Black pepper

1. In a large saucepan add olive oil, butter, garlic, onion, parsley and shallots
2. Cook slowly without colouring for 1 minute
3. Add the white wine and the cream
4. Bring to the boil
5. Wash the mussels well under cold water
6. Add the mussels to the pan and cover
7. Cook for 6 minutes stirring occasionally
8. Turn the heat off and leave to rest for 1 minute
9. Serve immediately

Coquille St Jacques au pommes
Scottish king scallops with a cox apple and parsnip veloute and parsnip crisp

Serve 4   Level 3

This is a delicate and subtle starter. Scottish scallops really are the best particularly from the West Coast of Scotland, the Hebrides, Orkney and Shetland. Thanks to early measures taken to prevent over fishing and the implementation of conservation restrictions on the size of scallops. Basically there are two types of scallop - queens and kings - and there is a great difference between them. King scallops are larger than queens and are diver caught. They provide a much more substantial piece of meat but at a price. Stay clear of queens which are small and after cooking end up looking like buttons and often rubbery. Never — repeat never – buy frozen scallops or ones that have been frozen, when defrosted and cooked they lose all their flavour, leaving a pan full of defrosted water.

You can prepare the parsnip veloute the day before

Ask your fishmonger for 12 Scottish king scallops don't settle for anything else

Clean and rinse with fresh water

4 cox apple peeled, corked and diced into small cubes

3 medium parsnips peeled and diced into small cubes

50g unsalted butter

Chopped chives

Salt and pepper

Put the butter in a medium saucepan and melt gently

Add the parsnips and sweat slowly for 3 minutes

Add the apple stir and cook slowly for 3 more minutes

Add 150ml of water

1. Bring to the boil and simmer for 20 minutes or until soft
2. Pour the mixture in the blender
3. Blend for 30 second or until the consistency of a thick soup
4. For the scallops use a medium size non stick pan
5. Use olive oil for frying the scallops
6. Warm the oil well put the scallops in the pan
7. Cook for 1 minutes then turn over cook for another minute
8. Then turn the heat off leave in the pan for another 2 or 3 minutes to gently finish the cooking process
9. Lightly salted and black pepper
10. Place 3 individual spoonful of parsnip and cox apple veloute on the plate
11. Place the scallops gently on top
12. Finish with finely chopped chives

Sardines au four, pommes de terre saffrane

Baked sardine fillets, saffron new potatoes and tomato salad with lemon and thyme dressing

Serves 4   Level 1

A fresh, summery and colourful starter. You need fresh sardines for this recipe, ask your fishmonger to fillet the sardines for you. Sardines are a group of several types of small oily fish related to the herring family. Sardines were named after the island of Sardinia, where they were once in abundance.

400g good quality new potatoes (use Jersey potatoes if in season)
8 fresh sardine, filleted
4 ripe plum tomatoes
1g of saffron
Olive oil
Juice of 2 lemons
Fresh thyme
100g sun-blush tomatoes
Flat leaf parsley, roughly chopped
Salt and pepper
100ml of dry white wine

Prepare the potatoes:

1. Cut the potatoes in 4 lengthways
2. Place in a small saucepan with salt and saffron
3. Cook until soft and set aside

Prepare the dressing:

4. Salt and pepper
5. Lemon juice
6. Stir until the salt is dissolved as the salt will not dissolve in oil
7. Add the white wine, olive oil and finely chopped thyme
8. Stir well and check the seasoning
9. Add the sun-blush tomatoes
10. Add the potatoes
11. Leave at room temperature

Cook the sardines:

12. Place the sardine fillets on a well-oiled baking tray
13. Season with salt and pepper
14. Sprinkle with fresh thyme and drizzle with olive oil
15. Bake in a moderate oven, 160*c for 10 minutes
16. Place the potato salad in the centre of the plates
17. Place the sardines on top and finish by drizzling over the remaining dressing

Soupe de poisons fume avec pain aux seigle
Smoked haddock and potato chowder served with rye bread

Serves 4   Level 1

This is a great soup recipe originally from Scotland.

1 naturally smoked haddock skinned and cut in small cubes

2 medium size potatoes peel and cut into small cubes

1 onion diced

2 cloves of garlic

Sprig of thyme

Chopped chives

250ml dry white wine

250ml double cream

250ml water of fish stock

50g unsalted butter

50g plain flour

1.   Melt the butter in a medium saucepan
2.   Add the onion, garlic, smoked haddock and potatoes
3.   Sweat slowly without colouring for 5 minutes
4.   Pour the white wine then the cream
5.   Bring to the boil then simmer for 10 minutes
6.   Add fish stock
7.   Bring to the boil again then simmer for 30 minutes
8.   Check for seasoning
9.   Add the chives and parsley
10.   Serve with lightly toasted rye bread and unsalted butter
       (see recipe in the bread section)

Anguille fume, salad de carrots sauce raifort
Smoked eel and grated carrot salad with horseradish cream

Serves 4   Level 1

Very popular starter at Mirabelle. It combines very simple ingredients but the combination of flavours is brilliant. You must use organic carrots for this recipe!

3 medium carrots - organic

1tsp of brown sugar

400g of natural smoked eel

6tbs olive oil

balsamic vinegar

freshly chopped coriander

4tbs of double cream

2tbs horseradish

1 spring onion finely chopped

1.   Peel and finely grate the carrots
2.   Add salt and pepper and the brown sugar
3.   Mix well then leave in the fridge for a couple of hours or overnight
4.   Cut the eel into long thin strips of 2cm wide
5.   The carrots will provide an orange liquid keep aside as you will use in the dressing
6.   Put the carrots in a small ring draining the excess of liquid
7.   Remove the ring and put the eel carefully on top of the carrot
8.   Mix the carrot juice, olive oil, balsamic vinegar, coriander, salt and pepper in a small container
9.   Drizzle around the carrots
10. Gently blend the cream with the horseradish, whip until stiff
11. Add the spring onion
12. Carefully place a spoonful of the cream on top of the smoked eel

Supreme de faisants aux cidre, puree de pommes
Poached breast of pheasant in sweet cider with apple and vanilla mash

Serves 4   Level 1

I love game because in Yorkshire we are blessed with amazing countryside providing us with a large amount of pheasant, woodcock, duck etc... Over the years we have built a great relationship with shoots around us and in return we make pates and sausages for them, a great way of doing business.

Pheasant is in season from November to February and your local butcher or farmers market will provide you with great birds. For this recipe you only need the breast so simply ask your butcher to prepare that for you.

4 pheasant breasts
1 litre of sweet cider
1 measure of calvados
1tsp of honey
4 large cooking apples
1 vanilla pod
100g unsalted butter
1tsp of gravy granules

Prepare the pheasant and cooking liquor:

1. Make sure the pheasant breasts are free from feathers and lead shot
2. Wash well under a tap and dry the breasts with kitchen roll
3. Add cider, honey and calvados to a medium pan
4. Split the vanilla pod in half with a small knives scrap the seeds into the liquor along with half of the pod (keep the other half for the mash)
5. Bring to the boil then reduce heat for 20 minutes
6. Add the pheasant and simmer for 15 minutes
7. Remove the breast of pheasant from the liquor
8. Bring liquor to the boil
9. Add the gravy granules to thicken the sauce
10. Cook for 5 minutes

Prepare the mash:

1. Peel and dice the apple (keep the equivalent of one diced apple aside for later)
2. Add the butter, apples and the vanilla pod to a medium size pan
3. Cook slowly for 10 minutes or until the apples soften, add the other apple you set aside
4. Cook for a further 5 minutes then stir well

To finish:

1. Place the apple mash in the centre of the plate
2. Place the pheasant on top
3. Pour a little of the liquor on the pheasant
4. Finish the dish with a thin slice of apple carefully place on the pheasant

Risotto de homard
Lobster risotto
Serve 4   Level 2

One of my favourite starters, full of flavour and texture. Whitby brings us an abundance of fresh shellfish, although lobster is expensive you only need one to make this recipe. Having said that, the more lobster you add the better. If you feel courageous then purchase live lobster otherwise buy one already cooked.

Fresh lobster:

1. Put the lobster in the freezer for at least one hour
2. To a large saucepan add 2 glasses of white wine, 1 chopped onion, 2 carrots, 2 cloves of garlic, 1 litre of water and a pinch of salt
3. Bring to the boil for ten minutes
4. Add the lobster to the saucepan and cook for 10 minutes, turn off the gas and leave to rest for a further 15 minutes
5. Remove the lobster
6. Reduce the liquor to about 750 ml

Cooked lobster:

1. Remove the shell from the lobster carefully saving all the bits of shell and juice
2. Place the shell and juice in a large saucepan together with 2tbs olive oil, 1 chopped onion, 2 cloves of garlic, 1tbs tomato puree, 2 glasses of white wine and 1 litre of fish stock
3. Bring to the boil for 20 minutes
4. Remove the shell from the saucepan and cook for a further 15 minutes

The risotto:

There are many theories as to how to make the perfect risotto but there are a couple of key points everyone agrees on. need the right type of rice and you need a decent hot stock.

If you can use Vialonenano, it is probably the best risotto rice on the market, however the Carnaroli and Arborio are both brilliant.

- **Arborio** - The most popular grain, it is large and rounded and has a wonderful creamy texture.
- **Carnaroli -** Fork's favourite grain - this long, elegant grain tends to hold its shape well even when completely cooked. It's a good choice if you find your risotto always turns a little mushy.
- **Vialonenano** - Now available in the UK, this is said to have the creamiest, smoothest texture of all.

1. Finely chop 1 onion, 2 carrots,1 red pepper, 3gloves of garlic,
2. Add 100ml of good olive oil to a large saucepan, add the finely chopped vegetables,
3. Cook very slowly without browning for 3 minutes
4. Add the rice and stir well for 1 minute
5. Add half of the lobster liquor to the mixture, stir well and keep an eye on the risotto as it will need more liquor
6. Add the lobster pieces and stir in well
7. If you run out of lobster liquor just add fish stock, chicken stock or simply water as a last resort
8. Taste the rice for tenderness, once cooked the rice will stay warm for a while so don't panic with your timing
9. Season to taste.

Viands et volailles
Meat and Poultry

Choosing meat carefully is important

If at all possible try not to buy frozen meat, you can't really see the quality of the cut and also it will be saturated with water that you will not be able to remove as the molecules of the meat have been broken down by the freezing process. It is also less likely that the meat is imported as most reputable suppliers in the UK do not freeze their meat

Local butcher

1. Introduce yourself to your local butcher. Use them regularly and they will look after you and your wallet. Good local butchers use local matured meat. They will also advise you as to which cut of meat is most suitable for what you want to cook.

2. If you buy from a local butcher who deals only in local meat, raised to high standards (all free-range, slaughtered in a tiny, well-run butchery within 5 miles of the farm, details of sourcing displayed in the shop ...) you will not only enjoy superior flavour and the comfort of knowing that the animal was well-treated when alive, but also you get a personal service.

3. When you balance quality against price it has to be your local butcher every time.

4. Buy the best grade of meat you can afford. Prime, Choice, Select, in that order; speak to your butcher, don't be afraid to ask questions.

5. Check the shop as it should advertise the fact that the meat is local, traceable.

6. Look for steaks with fine texture and firm to the touch.

7. Any other red meat you want, the colour should be a light cherry red, not deep red. And, by all means stay away from grey looking meat.

Supermarket:

1. When possible, buy from the butchers counter not the pre-packaged section.
2. Dry aging is considered better than wet aging but that may be a matter of taste, avoid meat that has no aging and is too fresh.
3. If you do buy packaged meat, stay away from any with excessive moisture, tears or that are past their sell by date.
4. Just because the label says Angus or farmed assure, doesn't mean anything, check the traceability of the meat.
5. If in doubt, preferably only buy meat from the UK or France as both countries have agreed standards of hygiene and welfare.
6. DO NOT BUY FROZEN MEAT, there is no need, we produce plenty of fresh meat and you can't check the quality or the age of frozen meat.
7. Avoid all the value meat if you can as supermarket value meat is just below average and often brought from abroad where provenance can be an issue.

Magret de canards tarte tatin d'ananas, sauce aux cerises et pamplemousse rose

Duck breast, pineapple tart tatin with pink grapefruit and black cherry sauce

Serves 6   Level 3

Duck breast is a brilliant alternative for dinner party, a succulent meat that can be served with a sweet or savoury sauce, widely available in supermarket now but often better purchased in your local butcher or farmers market. Try if you can to buy English of French. Gressingham or Barbary are two of the best to buy.

6 medium to small duck breasts, skin on

1 fresh pineapple if possible, tinned as a last result

400g short crust pastry

4 pink grapefruits

4 oranges

200g caster sugar

150g black cherries or tinned will do very well

50g unsalted butter

Pineapple tatin:

1. Peel the pineapple and slice into 8
2. Remove the centre with a sharp knife or a round cutter
3. Roll the pastry about 1 cm thick
4. Cut 6 round pieces of pastry using a saucer and a small sharp knife
5. Make sure the pastry will cover the pineapple
6. Set the pastry aside
7. In a large saucepan put 100g sugar, a knob of unsalted butter on a medium heat
8. Stir well until butter and sugar dissolve
9. Preheat the oven to 170*C
10. Grease a baking tray ready for the caramelised pineapple
11. Keep cooking until lightly golden
12. Add the pineapple, cook for about 1 minute each side
13. Place the caramelised pineapple on a buttered baking try
14. Place the pastry on top of the pineapple making sure you cover the pineapple well
15. Bake for 15 minutes or until the pastry is golden

The sauce:

1. Wash the oranges and pink grapefruits well
2. Peel the skin of 2 grapefruit and 2 orange
3. Cut very finely set aside
4. Cut and squeeze the oranges and grapefruit setting the juice aside
5. Remove and discard the stones of the black cherries
6. To a medium saucepan add 100g of caster sugar
7. Add the orange and pink grapefruit peel
8. Add 2 tbs of the juice
9. Cook on a low gas for 5 minutes or until sugar dissolves
10. Stir well until golden brown
11. Pour the juice into the caramelised peel
12. This must be done carefully

13. Leave to simmer for 10 minutes
14. Add the cherries
15. Stir occasionally

Prepare the duck breast:

1. To release excess fat from the duck, score each breast 6 times with a sharp knife
2. Season well with salt and pepper
3. Place the duck, skin down, in a large frying pan from cold
4. Bring slowly to a moderate heat, this releases excess fat and gives the skin a crisp golden colour
5. Cook for around 5 minutes occasionally checking the skin is not burning
6. Turn over and cook for 3 to 4 minute on a low heat
7. Place in the oven for 15 minutes at 160*C
8. Place the tarte tatin in the oven to warm
9. Bring the sauce to the boil
10. Remove the duck and leave it to rest
11. Slice the duck lengthways
12. Place the duck in the centre of the plate
13. Place the tarte tatin on the side
14. Finish the dish with the sauce on top of the duck
15. Do not put sauce on the tarte tatin, it will get soggy

Cassoulet de canard
Cassoulet of duck
Serves 6/8   Level 2

In the south of France the recipe for cassoulet has many different versions according to the town, from Toulouse to Carcassone, but they all have some ingredients in common; pork, duck, duck fat , garlic and beans. A great winter classic and this version is easy to prepare, you can even cook the dish several days before you need it.

Confit of 4 duck legs

6 good quality Toulouse sausages 'smoked is optional but good to use '

6 thick slices of good belly pork

65g of duck fat

1 head of garlic peeled and chopped

1 large onion chopped

2 carrots

1kg of haricot beans

Fresh thyme

2tbs of tomato puree

3 rashers of smoked bacon
   cut into fine strips

1 tin of chopped tomatoes

1. Soak the beans for 24 hours
2. Heat the duck fat in a large sauce pan
3. Add the onion, carrots, garlic and bacon
4. Cook and stir well until golden brown
5. Add the belly pork
6. Add the tomato puree and the chopped tomatoes
7. A pinch of salt
8. Add half litre of water
9. Stir well
10. Bring to the boil then simmer for 90 minutes or until the beans are soft and tender
11. Add water if the liquid is not covering the beans as haricot beans can absorb a lot of liquid
12. Add the Toulouse sausage and confit of duck
13. Simmer for a 45 minutes
14. Check for seasoning
15. The cassoulet should be golden brown with a thick consistency

Agneau a la marocaine cuit deux fois
Cooked twice fruity Moroccan lamb with olive oil couscous
Serves 6   Level 1

This is a one pan job with an incredible range of flavours and colour, North Africa offers so much in terms of spice and flavour but it seems to be little used in this country. You can make this as mild or as spicy as you like. Ask your butcher for shoulder or leg as there is not a great deal of difference in taste or flavour, however, shoulder is cheaper.

If you see this recipe elsewhere you may find that you are asked to pan fry the meat before cooking it fully or in some cases to flour coat the meat, all that does is add fat and flour to your dish without really adding flavour, it's also not very healthy.

We simply put the meat into flavoursome liquor, by doing so you are increasing the flavour of this dish. This is a dish you can cook the day before, in fact it's so much better cooked twice.

1.5kg of diced lamb shoulder
1 tin of chopped tomato
1 tin of chick peas
1tbs tomato puree
1 large onion
Cayenne pepper
2 gloves of garlic
3 courgettes
2 carrots
50g dried apricots
50g sultanas

1 red chilli - *optional*
1tbs harissa north African chilli paste
  nice but not essential
1tbs gravy
Olive oil
500g of plain couscous
A large oven proof dish or a large saucepan

The lamb:

1. Peel and roughly chop the onion, garlic, courgette and carrots
2. To a medium sauce pan add 2 tbs of olive oil
3. Add the vegetables and cook without colour for 5 minutes
4. Add 1tbs tomato puree and 1 tin of chopped tomato
5. Add 750ml of water
6. 1 tbs gravy granules
7. Stir well, bring to the boil
8. Add the raw meat to the liquor
9. Add the apricot and sultanas
10. Cook for about 1 hours stirring occasionally
11. Add a little water if the stock is reducing too much
12. Season to taste
13. Leave in the pan for an hour to rest
14. Place in the fridge until you need to eat
15. Simply reheat the lamb slowly for one hour at 170/180*C

The couscous:

1. Put the couscous in a medium heatproof bowl
2. Add a pinch of salt
3. Add 3 tbs of olive oil
4. Stir well
5. Leave for 5 minutes for the grain to absorb the oil
6. Add 200ml of boiling water to the couscous
7. Stir continuously for 2 minutes
8. Leave to rest for 3 minutes for the couscous to absorb the water
9. Serve immediately with the lamb
10. Finish with a little chopped chilli on top, optional

Porc au boudin et pommes

Grilled pork chop with black pudding, butternut squash mash and caramelised apple

Serves 4   Level 1

The choice of meat is paramount for the success of this dish; you must choose the meat wisely. Here are a few tips for when you pick a cut of pork:

Several different cuts can be called pork chops. All are great grilled or pan-fried. Note that thicker-cut pork chops with the bone still attached are the juiciest and most flavoursome. Request your butcher to leave the skin on, fat between the meat and the skin will keep the meat moist.

4 pork chops
1 large butternut squash
150g butter
8 thin slices of black pudding
4 apples
200ml pork gravy
Olive oil
4tbs brown sugar
Salt & pepper

For the pork and mash:

1. Peel and dice the squash into small cubes
2. Add the butter and the butternut squash to a medium saucepan
3. Cook slowly for 20 minutes, if too dry add a little water until soft enough to mash
4. Pan fry the black pudding in olive oil for 1 minute on both sides
5. Using a ring, place one slice of black pudding on the bottom, add a layer of the mash, top with another slice of black pudding
6. In a hot griddle pan cook the pork chop for 3 minutes on both sides, turn off the heat and cover with tin foil for a further 5 minutes
7. Deglaze the pan with a little cider and pork gravy
8. Reduce and season to taste

For the apples:

1. Heat some butter in a pan.
2. Dip one side of apple slices in sugar and cook (sugar-side down), in hot butter over a high heat for 3-4 minutes.
3. Sprinkle remaining sugar over apples.
4. Turn apples over and cook for 3-4 minutes longer. (Do not overcook or apples will be too soft)

Foie de veau aux choux
Grilled calves liver with white onion veloute, red onion marmalade and pancetta.

Serves 4   Level 2

Calves liver is very delicate in flavour and wonderfully smooth in texture. It is also full of iron and B vitamins, it goes well with with cognac and vanilla, smoked bacon or Jerusalem artichoke. Be careful not to overcook it as it will dry it out - remove it from heat while the center is still pink

Red onion marmalade can be used for several dish and keep well in the refrigerator
This red onion marmalade is a sweet-and-tangy condiment that can be used to top burgers, steaks, chicken or served with cheese, can also be a Substitute cranberry sauce

Red onion marmalade:
2 red onion
1 tbs redcurrant
1tbs vinegar
1tbs sugar

1. Peel and slice the red onions
2. Place in a saucepan with the red currant, vinegar and sugar
3. Cook on low heat for 20 minutes
4. Add a little water if necessary

For the white onion veloute:
3 medium size onions
1 pint of full cream milk
Nutmeg
100g unsalted butter
Salt and white pepper

1. Peel and chop the onions
2. Melt the butter and cook the onion without colouring them
3. Add the milk , salt, pepper and a pinch of nutmeg
4. Cook for 20 minutes and blend
5. Season to taste
6. Set aside

Crispy pancetta:
1. Place the pancetta in a oven tray and bake for 10 minutes at 180*C or until crispy
2. Leave to cool for a further 5 minutes before using

The calves liver:
In a hot griddle pan cook the calves liver for 1 minute on both sides and season to taste. To serve simply pour the veloute onto the centre of a warm plate, place the calves liver on top, add the marmalade to one side and add the pencetta. If you like you could add a fried onion ring.

Poulet grille aux citron
Char grilled lemon and coriander chicken with wild rice salad
Serves 6   Level 1

This recipe was created as a fusion of Chinese and Asian cuisine, it can be served hot with rice or cold with a rice salad or couscous, either way and it is great for dinner on a long summers evening.

Use good quality rice, organic brown rice or wild rice are perfect. For this recipe you will need a griddle pan or a BBQ or you can use skewers instead and bake the chicken in a moderate oven, 170° for 20 minutes then pour the sauce over the chicken and cook at 150° for a further 10 minutes.

5 breasts of free-range chicken
1 tin of Chinese lemon sauce
3 unwaxed lemons, you will need the juice and the peel
1 onion
1 bunch of fresh coriander
400g wild rice
1 red pepper
1 tin sweet corn
1 red onion
Olive oil
Balsamic vinegar

1. In a medium sauce pan pour the lemon sauce. Fill tin with water place the top back on then shake well, pour the water into the pan
2. Add juice of 2 freshly squeezed lemons
3. Peel and finely slice the onion, add to the saucepan
4. Bring gently to the boil then leave to simmer
5. Slice the chicken into 6 lengthways strips, if using skewers cut into large cubes
6. Preheat and lightly oil the griddle pan
7. Place the chicken on the hot griddle pan
8. Cook for at least 3 minutes, turn over and cook for a further 3 minutes
9. Remove from the pan and place in the lemon sauce
10. Carry on the process until all chicken is in the lemon sauce
11. Simmer for 15 minutes
12. Add half of the bunch of coriander, roughly chopped and stir gently
13. Leave to rest for 15 minutes
14. You can then place it in the fridge to be served as a salad or serve immediately
    (secret for this dish is minimum movement to the chicken on the griddle, brown well)

You can prepare the salad in advance:
1. Cook the rice, rinse well, place in a colander, ensure the rice is cooked but not soggy
2. Chop the pepper and red onion into small cubes
3. Place 4 tbs balsamic vinegar in a mixing bowl
4. Add juice of 1 lemon
5. Season with salt and pepper
6. Add 8 tbs of olive oil
7. Pour the rice into the dressing and stir well

To serve:
1. Place a large tbs of rice on the plate
2. Place the chicken on the side and finish with chopped coriander

Poisons et fruits de mer
Fish and shellfish

I love cooking fish, I always have done partly because it is so much more challenging to get right. At our restaurant we get our fish from Whitby and Redcar, some of the best fish in the country arrive here every morning

In parallel with most other UK fishing ports - The Whitby Fishing Fleet has been reduced by over half in recent years due due to conservation measures taken to keep fishing sustainable for future generations. As a result, the remaining skippers all ensure that their catch, which is heavily restricted by quotas and limited fishing days at sea, is of the highest quality. This means we get great fish straight from the sea to our kitchen.

Imagine your fish coming straight from the sea, into the boat, onto the auction market, then straight over the road to our restaurant it's a dream come true for most chefs.

In the past, much of this fish has made its way to Billingsgate Fish Market, where discerning individuals, restaurateurs and top chefs demand the best. The French are also extremely partial to Whitby fish and most of it is shipped to Rungis market.

Due to severe demand fish like sea bass, turbot and of course salmon is now farmed. Nothing wrong with that. The price is lower than the line caught or wild, but the flavour is somewhat lacking.

We are privileged in Yorkshire to have such great fishing and the fish is unlike anywhere else: plaice, lemon sole, turbot, Dover sole, monk fish, squid, red mullet, sardines, hake. Whitby is also famous for crab and lobster, again some of the best in the country. Fresh shellfish: lobster, langoustine, dressed crab, boiled crab, king and queen scallops, razor clams, prawns, mussels, whelks... and more.

Here are a few tips to recognise fresh fish:

How to select, buy and cook fish and shellfish
1. Only purchase fish and seafood at reputable markets.
2. Don't buy anything more than one day or at most a couple of days old.
3. Avoid fish or seafood that has been in a display case for extended periods, even if it is on ice. If you are unsure, ask how fresh it is.
4. The flesh of fresh fish should always be firm and should adhere firmly to the bone.
5. Fresh fish should be firm and the flesh should spring back when touched.
6. Smell the fish. It should have a "fresh sea" aroma to it - NO STRONG ODORS. If it has a strong "fishy" smell, it is not fresh!
7. If you are shopping at a supermarket buy fresh fish or seafood on your way out of the store, take it directly home, and cook it within 24 hours.
8. Keep the fish as cold as possible until you are ready to cook it, store seafood in the coldest part of your refrigerator. When you are ready to cook the fish, rinse it with cold water.

Cuts and names:

Fresh fish or seafood is marketed in a number of ways. The best way to buy fish for preparation is in fillet or steak form. Fillets are normally bone free and steaks are usually cut into serving portion sizes making your prep time shorter. Don't hesitate to ask the fishmonger to prepare your fish as you need it, this will save you time and effort.

1. **Whole Round** - Means that the fish are exactly as they came from the water. The eyes should be clear, the gills bright red, and the skin shiny with tightly clinging scales. Allow one pound per serving.
2. **Dressed or Pan Dressed Fish** - Fish that have scales and entrails removed, and usually also with head, tail, and fins removed. Allow one-half pound per serving.
3. **Steaks** - Ready-to-cook width wise slices of large fish. Allow one-third to one-half pound per serving.
4. **Fillets** - Ready-to-cook sides of fish cut lengthwise form the backbone. Allow one-half pound per serving.

Cooking fish – the 10 minute rule:
1. The biggest mistake most people make in cooking fish is to overcook it.
2. Regardless of the fish or the cooking method (grilling, frying, baking, poaching, steaming or broiling), there is one basic rule that can be followed. Measure the fish, whether it is whole, in steaks, or in fillets, at its thickest point. Then cook exactly ten minutes for each measured inch of thickness.
3. If you are baking fish in sauce or an aluminium foil package with the edges sealed, allow a little extra time for the heat to penetrate the foil - five minutes more for fresh fish.

*Note: times are guidelines

Remember: fish will continue to cook after it is removed from the heat source. Do not overcook.

Trio de coquilles St Jacques
Trio of wild caught sea scallop
Serves 4   Level 4

Ravioli de Coquilles St Jacques
Scallop ravioli
Risotto de Coquilles St Jacques
Scallop risotto
Coquilles St Jacques aux pommes douce
Pan-fried scallop with cox apple and parsnip puree

This is one of my signature dishes, it took almost a year to perfect the recipe but the outcome is, if I say so myself, simply outstanding in both colour and flavour. This is a complicated dish but not impossible to do however each of the 3 recipes can be achieved on their own with great results. These can be served individually or as a trio.

12 good quality scallops, ask your fish monger to clean and trim the scallops, remove the orange muscle off the scallop apart from four, save the orange muscle for the risotto

Ravioli de Coquilles St Jacques
Scallop ravioli

Ask your fish monger to clean and trim 12 good quality scallops. Remove the orange muscle from all but 4 scallops and save for the risotto.

250g pasta dough

1 bunch of flat parsley

1tbs olive oil

1 egg white

1. Using a pasta machine roll out a strip large enough to cut out 8 x 5cm round
2. Place the 4 scallops in a small mixing bowl add a pinch of salt and pepper
3. Add 1tbs olive oil
4. Add 1tbs of finely chopped parsely
5. Mix gently until the scallops are well coated with the seasoning
6. Place 1 scallop in each of the 4 circles of pasta dough
7. Gently brush the circle with egg white, this process will seal the scallop ravioli
8. Place the other circle over the scallop pressing well around the edges
9. Carry on the process with the next 3
10. Place in a well-floured tray *(can be frozen until ready to serve)*
11. Plunge in a pan of salted boiling water and cook for 3 minutes
12. Drain well serve straight away

Risotto de Coquilles St Jacques
Scallop risotto

4 scallops

The orange muscle from the other scallops

200gr Arborio rice

1 onion

1 carrot

2 garlic gloves

1 glass of white wine

250ml fish stock

1. Peel and finely chop the onion, carrot and garlic
2. In a large saucepan place 3 tbs olive oil
3. Add the onion, carrot and garlic
4. Cook gently without browning
5. Add the orange part of the scallop
6. Cook for a further 3 minutes
7. Add 1 glass of white wine
8. Stir well and simmer for 5 minutes
9. Adding fish stock as necessary
10. Cook for 15 minutes or taste the rice, it should still be a little crunchy in the centre
11. Serve straight away or leave to cool for 20 minutes then refrigerate until needed

Coquilles St Jacques aux pommes douce
Pan-fried scallop with cox apple and parsnip puree

4 scallops with the orange muscle

4 English cox apple

300g parsnips

50g unsalted butter

Salt and pepper

1. Peel and chop in small cubes the apple and parsnips
2. Melt the butter in a medium pan
3. Add the apple and parsnip
4. Cook for 3 minutes without browning
5. Cover the mixture with water
6. Cook for 20 minutes
7. When the parsnips are soft enough place the mixture in a blender for 1 minute or until reduced to a puree
8. Set aside until needed
9. In a small non-stick frying pan place a knob of butter and a tbs of olive oil
10. Place the scallops in the centre of the pan and cook gently
11. Season with salt and pepper
12. Cook for 1 minute then turn over
13. Cook for a further 1 minute then turn the heat off
14. Leave in the pan for 3-4 minutes

Filet de sole au crab, epinard et beurre blanc
Sole fillets filled with Whitby crab over wilted spinach
Serves 3   Level 4

This recipe is a real tribute to our coastal fisherman best quality British fish with a French twist.

4 large lemon sole - ask your fish monger to skin the sole
1 large dressed crab or 200gr of fresh crab meat
freshly chopped chives
2tbs mayonnaise
Salt and pepper
200g fresh spinach
2 finely chopped shallots
4tbs of white wine
2tbs of white wine vinegar
4tbs double cream
200g unsalted butter

1. Preheat oven to 170*C
2. Put the crab meat in a mixing bowl, season well with salt and pepper
3. Add 2tbs of mayonnaise and the chives, mix well
4. Place the sole on a flat surface, season well with salt and pepper
5. Place the crab meat in the centre of the sole then roll the sole
6. In a shallow oven dish lightly drizzle with olive oil
7. Place the sole in the dish and add 4 tbs of water or white wine
8. Place in the oven for 20 minutes

Beurre blanc:

1. Place the shallots and the white wine in a small sauce pan
2. Bring to the boil and reduce for 2 minutes
3. Cut the butter into small cubes and add slowly to the hot mixture
4. Whisk constantly until the butter is melted

To finish:

1. Wash the spinach well and place in a large pan with 2 tbs of beurre blanc
2. Cook gently until wilted
3. Place the spinach in the centre of the plate
4. Place the sole on top of the spinach
5. Pour 4 tbs of beurre blanc over the sole
6. Finish with chopped chives

Turbot vapeur, risotto de homard
Oven steamed wild caught turbot with lobster risotto
Serves 4   Level 3

You can choose other types of fish for this recipe as the risotto is a great way of serving fish.
I have chosen turbot because this highly prized flatfish has firm, lean, white flesh with a mild flavour. I rate Turbot in the same category as the highly regarded Dover Sole. Turbot can reach 30 pounds but are generally marketed at weights closer to 3 to 6 pounds as the larger ones are sold to restaurants or sent to the continent.

4 fillets of skinned turbot
1 live lobster
500g Arborio rice
1 carrot
1 medium onion
2 cloves of garlic
100 fresh or frozen peas

Cooking the lobster from live:
1. Put the lobster in the freezer for at least one hour before starting.
2. In a large sauce pan pour 2 glasses of white wine 1 chopped onion, 2 carrots, 2 cloves of garlic, 1 litre of water a pinch of salt
3. Bring this to the boil for ten minutes
4. Then put the lobster in the saucepan and cook for 10 minutes, turn off the gas and leave to rest for a further 15 minutes
5. Remove the lobster from the liquor and reduce to about 750 ml

Cooking shop bought lobster:

1. Remove the shell from the lobster carefully saving all the bits of shell and juice
2. Place all the shell and juice in a large saucepan together with 2 tbs olive oil, 1 onion chopped, 2 glove of garlic, 1tbs tomato puree, 2 glasses of white wine and 1 litre of fish stock
3. Bring to the boil for 20 minutes
4. Then remove the shell from the saucepan and cook for a further 15 minutes

Cooking the risotto:

1. Finely chop 1 onion, 2 carrots,1 red pepper, 3 cloves of garlic
2. Put 100ml of good olive oil in a large sauce pan, add the finely chopped vegetables
3. Cook very slowly without browning for 3 minutes
4. Add the rice and stir well for one minute
5. Add half of the lobster liquor to the mixture, stir well and keep an eye on the risotto constantly as it will need more liquor
6. Add the lobster pieces and stir well
7. If you run out of lobster liquor just add fish stock, chicken stock or simply water as a last resort
8. Taste the rice for tenderness, once cooked the rice will stay warm for a while so don't panic with your timing
9. Season to taste
10. Whilst the risotto is cooking
11. Drizzle olive oil in a small oven tray
12. Place the turbot in the tray and add 4tbs of water or white wine
13. Cook for 10 minutes 180°C
14. Spoon risotto onto a plate and place turbot on top

Fletan au saumon fume
Grilled halibut fillet with smoked salmon and broad bean broth
Serves 4   Level 1

I created this recipe from a chat with my friend David Clough. David is passionate about smoking fish and we have spent many hours experimenting with hot and cold smoking. Using smoked fish in a recipe usually takes over the whole of the dish, however if you are using smoked salmon as part of a sauce it brings a light but intense flavour to the rest of the dish.

Halibut is a versatile fish and is considered to be mild in flavour therefore it needs a good accompaniment, smoked salmon brings a light smoke flavour to the beurre blanc and the broad beans brings colour and texture to the recipe.

4 pieces of halibut - skinned
150g of smoked salmon
2 finely chopped shallots
1 small glass of white wine
2tbs of white wine vinegar
4tbs double cream
200g unsalted butter
150g fresh or frozen broad beans
100g smoked salmon
Olive oil
Salt and pepper
Smoked paprika

1. Wash and dry the halibut well, place in a small flat dish, add a drizzle of olive oil, salt and pepper and a pinch of smoked paprika
2. Preheat your griddle pan in a low gas
3. Coat the fish well with oil and seasoning, cover and leave in in the fridge until needed
4. Broad beans have a very thick skin, with your finger remove and discard the skin and keep the beans aside until needed
5. In a medium saucepan place the glass of white wine, shallots, white wine vinegar and finely the smoked salmon
6. Bring to the boil and simmer for 2 minutes
7. Add the beans and the cream
8. Cook for a further 2 minutes
9. Cut the butter into small cubes and add to the hot mixture
10. Stir constantly until the butter has melted
11. Heat the non-stick griddle pan (very hot) and place the 4 pieces of halibut gently in the pan
12. Reduce the heat a little, leave to cook for 3 minutes then turn over and cook for a further 3 minutes
13. Turn off the heat and leave the fish in the pan for another 4 minutes as it will carry on cooking
14. Serve immediately with the sauce over the fish

Curry de lotte aux crevettes Thailandaise, riz a la coriander
Thai red curry of monkfish, prawns and coriander rice

Serves 4   Level 2

A revelation to me later on in my cooking voyage as I knew little about Thai food until I met Fred Martin the landlord of the Ash Tree Inn. Fred was as passionate about food as I am and for a short time I worked with Fred. We talked about food all day long and we developed dishes that I frequently use to this day.

Sadly, Fred passed away a few years ago. I still miss him and our food talk over a glass of ale. Here's to you Fred!

This is a colourful fish dish with a hint of spice. Monkfish is a delicate fish therefore does not need a lot of heat however if you like your food spicy just increase the curry paste. Monkfish is an expensive fish all year round but its flavour and lack of bones makes it a great fish to eat Ask your fishmonger to cut 3 small pieces per person.

12 pieces of trimmed and cleaned monkfish
200g of fresh or frozen prawns
1 finely chopped onion
1 chopped red pepper
4 chopped garlic gloves
1 finely chopped lemon grass
1 bunch of chopped coriander
2tbs of Thai red curry paste
2 tins of coconut milk
200g of Thai rice or basmati rice
2tbs olive oil
2tbs olive oil

For the sauce:

1. In a saucepan place the olive oil, onion, red pepper, garlic and curry paste
2. Cook slowly for 2 minutes to dissolve and cook the curry paste
3. Add the coconut milk, lemon grass and coriander
4. Simmer gently for 10 minutes
5. Add the pieces of monkfish and cook for 10 minutes
6. Add the prawns cook for a further 5 minutes then turn off the heat
7. Leave the pan to rest for another 10 minutes before you serve it

For the rice:

1. Bring a pan of water to the boil, this should be 1 times the volume of rice
2. Add a pinch of salt
3. Add the rice and cook slowly for 15 minutes
4. When the rice is nearly cooked add a good handful of coriander
5. Mix well and leave to infuse for 10 minutes before serving
6. Using a shallow bowl place the rice in the middle and the fish around it making sure you provide plenty of sauce
7. Finish with chopped coriander

Loup de mer aux poireaux, moules et safran

Pan-fried line caught sea bass fillets with leek, mussel and saffron broth

Serves 4   Level 2

You can now find sea bass in most supermarkets; it is likely to be farmed. For this recipe try to go to an independent fishmonger as he will often have wild, line caught sea bass. Farmed sea bass comes mainly from Greece and is reasonably cheap, but is not the superior quality of wild sea bass. You also need fresh mussels for this recipe, these are in season from September to April.

4 sea bass fillets - ask the fishmonger to fillet and bone the sea bass

1kg fresh mussels – wash thoroughly in cold water

1g of saffron

1 medium leek

3 chopped garlic gloves

2 chopped shallots

2tbs of flat parsley

250ml of double cream

Olive oil

250ml white wine

Unsalted butter

4tbs of plain flour

1tbs of smoked paprika

Cook the broth:

1. In a large sauce pan place 20g of butter and 2tbs olive oil
2. Add the chopped garlic and shallots and cook for 1 minute without browning
3. Add the mussels to the pan
4. Add the white wine
5. Cover and bring to the boil for 4 minutes
6. Turn off the heat and leave to rest in the pan for 15 minutes
7. Strain the liquor into a bowl and set aside
8. Keep 8 mussels in the shell for the presentation
9. Remove the shell from the rest of the mussels and place in the liquor
10. Chop the leek into small cubes and wash well
11. In a medium pan add 20g butter
12. Add the chopped leek and cook gently for 3 minutes
13. Add the saffron, the liquor and the cream
14. Simmer for 15 minutes

Cook the sea bass:

1. Wash and dry the sea bass fillets
2. Place 4tbs of plain flour and 1tbs of smoked paprika in a plate or shallow dish
3. Add a pinch of salt and mix well
4. Place the sea bass fillet in the flour mixture making sure the fillet is well coated
5. Using a large frying pan
6. Add 30g of butter and 3tbs of olive oil and place under medium heat
7. Once the butter is melted place the sea bass fillet in the pan skin side down
8. Cook slowly for 3 minutes then carefully turn over
9. Cook for a further 3 minutes then turn the heat off and leave in the pan for 3 minutes
10. Check the broth for seasoning
11. Add the chopped parsley and the mussels with the shells on
12. Place the sea bass in the middle of the plate and pour over the broth

Tagine de rouget aux chorizo, couscous
Tagine of red mullet with chorizo and coucous
Serves 4   Level 2

You will need 2 fillets per person. Ask your fish monger to fillet, descale and bone the fish. Red mullet is usually small therefore does not require much cooking.

8 fillets red mullet

8 slices of spicy chorizo

Olive oil

Sea salt

1tbs sultanas

200g organic couscous

1 red chilli

1 spring onion

1 clove of garlic

50g chopped sun blush tomatoes

Preheat oven to 220* C gas 7

Place the red mullet fillet on a lightly oiled baking tray skin side up

Place a slice of chorizo on top of each fillet - optional

Brush a little oil on the fillet and season with sea salt

Chop the garlic place the garlic in the baking tray around the red mullet

1. In a medium bowl place the couscous the chopped sun blush tomato and the sultanas
2. Pour 4tbs of olive oil and a sprinkle of sea salt
3. Stir well and leave for 5 minutes to enable flavours to mix
4. Pour on 250ml of boiling water over the couscous
5. Stir constantly with a fork
6. Add the chopped chilli and the chopped spring onion
7. Stir again until the couscous is cooked
8. Taste for seasoning
9. Put a plate on top of the bowl whilst the red mullet is cooking
10. Bake the red mullet in a hot oven for 6 minutes
11. Spoon the couscous into a warm tagine dish and place the fish on top

Ragout de poisons
Fish stew/pie

Serves 4   Level 1

Many variations of this dish have been made over the years but this one has a twist to the finish which will surprise your guests when you serve it. You will carefully place mushy peas in the bottom of the dish then place the fish on top, then the sauce, finish with mash potatoes and gruyere cheese. The mushy peas add another smooth texture to the fish pie as well as flavour, a great classic with a twist.

150g fresh salmon skinned and boned
150g halibut skinned and boned
100g smoked salmon in strip
50g sliced mushrooms
50g chopped onion
1 litre of organic full cream milk
100g unsalted butter
50g plain flour
150g mushy peas
4 large potatoes
chopped parsley
150g grated gruyere

1. In a medium saucepan add the milk, chopped onion, sliced mushrooms and the smoked salmon
2. Bring to the boil and leave the flavour to infuse for 15 minutes
3. Peel and cook the potatoes in lightly salted water
4. Place the halibut and salmon in the milk and bring to the boil for 5 minutes
5. Turn the heat off and again leave to rest for 10 minutes whilst you prepare the mashed potatoes
6. Using a sieve retrieve the fish from the liquor
7. In a medium pan add 50g butter and melt gently on a low flame
8. Using a whisk add 50g of flour
9. Stir well and cook for 2 minutes
10. Add the liquor and stir well until thickened
11. Add chopped parsley
12. Season to taste
13. Place the mushy peas carefully on the bottom of the dish
14. Crumble the fish on top
15. Pour the sauce on top of the fish
16. Leave for 30 minutes or over night until the sauce settles and cools otherwise as you spoon on the mash the sauce will come to the top as you apply pressure to the fish
17. Place the mash on top starting from the outside first then finish with the middle
18. Sprinkle with cheese and bake for 30 minutes at 170°C gas 7
19. It has a better finish if you use individual dishes as you can serve it with a side salad on the plate, rye bread and unsalted butter

Gibiers et des oiseaux sauvages
Game and wild birds

Choosing and cooking game:

Most game like wild birds are simply brilliant roasted, deglazed the caramelised juice in the roasting tin with red or white wine, depending on the bird add wild mushrooms, salt and pepper, that's it really.

For strong game like venison or hare you will need a rich sauce to match the original flavour. Try to use wild game if you can but nowadays most game is farmed simply to satisfy demand as well sustainability.

Hate it or love it, you simply can't ignore sustainable farming provided it is done with the welfare of the animal in mind. There is nothing wrong with farmed game particularly venison.

Don't hang game or buy game that has been hanged, this is a thing of the past, it smells horrid and little is achieved by the process. Fresh game should have an attractive colour and hardly any smell.

Try not to buy birds that have been shot in the breast as it has probably been reduced to mush. The flesh should be firm and the skin dry. Britain has an incredible variety of game and birds unlike France where it is rapidly becoming extinct due largely to over enthusiastic Frenchmen who shoot on sight just about anything that flies or jumps. This has dramatically reduced the wild life population.

At our restaurant, we are close to several pheasant, pigeon and grouse shoots and we use wild and farmed game depending on the quality and sustainability.

General advice on game:

Because game is a lean meat it needs to be cooked with care. Unlike our chicken and duck, no two birds or animals will have had exactly the same diet or exercise. It is important to pick younger birds and animals as they are often tender. It is crucial that you buy game from a good game dealer.

Sanglier aux choux et lard fume
Wild boar steak served with buttered cabbage and smoked bacon baked apple

Serves 4   Level 1

This is a very simple but flavoursome dish. Wild boar, as the name implies is simply a wild pig therefore needs to be cooked just like pork, it has so much more flavour than pork it is almost how pork should taste. Wild boar is actually extinct in Great Britain and is mainly farmed like pork however wild boar thrives in France and Spain so much so that they are becoming a nuisance. Recipes for pork can be used for wild boar.

4 wild boar steaks, about 200g

1 large cabbage

150g smoked bacon or pancetta

100g unsalted butter

Olive oil

200ml red wine

1tbs gravy granules

Salt and pepper

Handful of wild mushrooms

4 red apples

1tbs honey

For the boar:

1. Wash the 4 apples and with a small knife prick the skins, this will help baking the apple without cracking,
2. Put in the oven 170°C for 20 minutes
3. Wash and finely chop the cabbage and set aside
4. To a large saucepan add 40g butter and 1tbs of olive oil
5. Place the steak in the pan and leave to cook for 8 minutes
6. Season with salt and pepper
7. In a large sauce pan place 60g butter
8. Add the chopped pancetta and cook until brown and crispy
9. Add the raw cabbage to the pan and stir well
10. Add 4tbs of water and another 25g of butter
11. Turn the steak over and cook for a further 8 minutes on a low heat
12. Remove the steak from the frying pan
13. Pour the red wine into the pan, add the mushrooms and stir to mix with the flavours of the wild boar
14. Add a teaspoon of gravy granules
15. Stir well then place the steak back in the pan
16. Simmer for 2 minutes then serve with the buttered cabbage, apple, mushrooms and the red wine sauce

Chevreuil Aux poires roti
Venison steak with a pear and roasted butternut squash
Serves 4   Level 2

Pear and butternut squash are simply a wonderful combination. As the venison steak is lean and tender you will have a great flavour in the sauce too. Serve with lightly cooked green beans, this dish is really great for a dinner party.

Four types of venison are available in the UK, Red, Fallow, Roe and Farmed deer.

The red deer is the largest of the four and tends to have the strongest and richest flavour. The roe dear is small, delicate and the most tender of the three wild species. The fallow deer seem to come somewhere in between when it comes to flavour and size.

For this recipe you will need steaks from the rump of the loin.

4 venison steak
4 firm pears
1 lemon
4tbs sugar
4 shallots
Olive oil
3tbs of sherry or Madeira
Gravy granules of 500ml beef stock
Unsalted butter
1 large butternut squash

1. Peel and take the core from the pear
2. Keep the peel for later
3. Poach pear in 500ml of water with juice of 1 lemon until soft
4. In a medium saucepan add 3tbs olive oil and the chopped shallots, cook for 3 minutes then add the peel from the pear
5. Add the stock or 500ml of water with 2tbs of beef granules
6. Simmer for 15 minutes
7. Strain into another saucepan, leave to simmer until ready to serve
8. Wash the butternut squash, cut into large chunks removing all seeds
9. In a lightly oiled baking tray place the butternut squash and cook for 45 minutes at 180°C
10. Pre-heat a heavy frying pan or griddle pan
11. Gently season the steak with salt and pepper
12. Lightly oil the pan, then fry the steak for 4 to 5 minutes on each side depending how you prefer it (4 to 5 minutes per side should give you a pink to medium rare)
13. Remove the meat and place the pear in the pan whilst it still very hot
14. Quickly reheat the pears
15. Remove the butternut squash from the oven
16. Serve on a large plate with the pear, butternut and the meat, whole or sliced
17. Pour the sauce over the steak

Ragout de faisants tarte au figues
Pot roast pheasant with a savoury fig tart and sloe gin sauce

Serves 4   Level 2

Pheasant:

2 pheasants cut in half lengthways - ask your butcher to prepare for you

45g unsalted butter

Olive oil

3 shallots chopped

2 stick of celery diced

2 carrots diced

1 onion chopped

1 apple chopped

300ml of chicken stock

5tbs of sloe gin

5tbs port

Fig tart:

4 fresh figs

50g redcurrant jelly

150g puff pastry

1 egg yolk

For the pheasant:

1. In a sauté pan heat the butter with 2tbs olive oil
2. Brown each pheasant piece, skin first, for 3 minutes then turn over and season lightly
3. Once brown place the pheasant in a roasting tin. Repeat the same process until all 4 halves are done
4. Place the pheasant in the oven for 30 minutes at gas mark 5 160° C
5. Add the vegetables and fruit to the sauté pan
6. Cook the vegetables for 5 minutes
7. Add the chicken stock, port and sloe gin to the pan, stir well until the stock is boiling
8. Reduce the heat and leave to simmer until reduced by half
9. Remove the pheasant from the oven
10. Leave 10 minutes to rest
11. Bring the stock to the boil
12. Add 50g redcurrant jelly
13. Stir well and season

The fig tart:

1. Roll the puff pastry and cut into 4 with a round pastry cutter or simply use a cup or a small saucer
2. Place the pastry in a baking tray
3. Brush the pastry with egg yolk
4. Slice the fig in thick pieces
5. Place onto the pastry
6. Brush the fig with recurrent jelly
7. Bake for 12 minutes

Serving:

1. Place the pheasant on a large plate, add the fig tart
2. Finish with the sauce on the side

Pintades a l'orange et Madeire
Guinea fowl with Madeira and spiced oranges
Serves 6   Level 2

Guinea fowl is basically wild chicken, originating from West Africa, the bird has dark plumage mottled with white and is now raised for food in many parts of the world. It has a very light and nutty flavour.

1tbsp oil

25g butter

2kg guinea fowl or pheasant

225g shallots or button onions, peeled with the root end trimmed

225g streaky bacon, cut into thin strips or lardons

4 tangerines, halved

50g kumquats, halved

2.5 cm (1 in) fresh root ginger piece, peeled and coarsely grated

2 garlic cloves, crushed

2tbsp plain flour

300 ml Madeira

600 ml fresh chicken stock

Cinnamon stick

Juice of 1 tangerine

3tbsp redcurrant jelly

200g vacuum-packed chestnuts, optional

Chopped fresh flat-leaf parsley to garnish

Couscous to serve

1. Preheat oven to 170°C/150°C fan oven/ Gas Mark 3
2. Heat the oil and butter in a deep flameproof casserole. Add the guinea fowl in batches and cook until the skin is browned before turning and browning on the other side. Remove with a slotted spoon and set aside
3. Add the shallots, bacon, tangerine halves and kumquats to the pan and cook, stirring, until brown
4. Stir in the ginger and garlic and cook for 1 minute
5. Stir in the flour, Madeira and stock
6. Return the joints to the casserole, then add the cinnamon stick, tangerine juice and redcurrant jelly
7. Bring to the boil; cover and cook in the oven for 50 to 60 minutes or until tender. (The cooking time depends on the thickness of the joints, not their weight, so return it to the oven, if necessary)
8. Discard the cinnamon stick
9. Lift the guinea fowl out of the sauce, cover with foil and keep warm
10. In a small pan, bring the sauce to the boil, add the chestnuts, if using, and bubble for 10 minutes or until reduced by half
11. Pour over the guinea fowl, to serve
12. Garnish with the parsley and serve with couscous on the side

Ragout de faisants aux noix et champignons sauvage
Ragout of pheasant with walnuts and wild mushrooms

Serves 6   Level 2

The pheasant:
2 young oven-ready pheasants or guinea fowls

25g softened butter

5tbsp sherry vinegar

225g onion, chopped

175g carrots, chopped

175g celery sticks, diced

3 fresh bay leaves

15g dried porcini mushrooms

4tbsp mushroom ketchup

450ml red wine or wine and port mixed

600ml fresh chicken or game stock

175g wild or flat black mushrooms, sliced

125g walnut halves

Fresh thyme to garnish

For the kneaded butter:
50g butter softened

40g plain flour

1. Preheat the oven to 230°C/2I0°C fan oven/Gas Mark 8
2. Smear pheasants all over with the softened butter
3. Lay on their sides in a large roasting tin and roast for 15 minutes (guinea fowl for 20 minutes)
4. Turn the birds over and roast for a further 15 minutes (guinea fowl for 20 minutes)
5. Remove from the oven - they should be quite rare
6. When cool enough to handle, remove the legs and cut the breast off the bone
7. Place the legs under a preheated grill and cook for 4 to 5 minutes each side
8. Arrange the legs in the bottom of a 2.8 litre shallow, ovenproof dish, place the breast meat on top. Cool, then cover and chill for 3 hours or overnight
9. Meanwhile, break up the carcasses and place in a large saucepan
10. Add the sherry vinegar to the roasting tin, scraping the bottom to dislodge any sediment
11. Then add to the carcass stock pot with the next eight ingredients
12. Slowly bring to the boil, turn down the heat and simmer for 1 hour
13. Strain the stock into a jug, discard the vegetables and herbs, return the stock to the pan. Bring to a fast boil and reduce to 750ml and season well
14. Make the kneaded butter by mixing the butter and flour to a smooth paste
15. Gradually whisk the kneaded butter into the stock, bring to the boil and bubble until syrupy
16. Add the mushrooms and walnuts to the sauce, then cool quickly, cover and chill until the game is ready to serve
17. To serve, reduce the oven temperature to 180°C/160°C fan oven/Gas Mark 4
18. Reheat the sauce then pour over the game and cover
19. Place in the oven and cook for about 1 hour or until hot in the centre
20. Garnish with sprigs of thyme

Nos desserts
Desserts

Desserts should be a visual and sensual end to a meal. Desserts should be fun, bold and fancy, pure pleasure and should never be attempted with low fat stuff!! It's all cream and butter!!!

Early records show that from the Egyptians to the crusaders there is evidence of honey mixed with rice or sugar mixed with flour and eggs to create some kind of desserts. But it's the French and Italian Renaissance chefs who are credited with perfecting the art of dessert making, they have also perfected pastries such as puff and choux bun. 17th and 18th century chefs introduced several new recipes, including brioche, Napoleons, cream puffs and eclairs. Antonin Careme (1784-1833) is said to have elevated French pastry to an art form. In Central and Eastern Europe, sweet yeast-breads and cakes share a parallel history. It is fair to say that most recipes we use now have been created over 100 years ago.

Although the Paris pastry chef's guild did not record its first constitution until 1440, there may well have been pastry specialties before that date. In today's world, pastries and cakes are a multi-million pound business and pastry chefs are real artists pushing the boundaries of flavours and the blending of ingredients.

My first encounter with serious desserts was at the restaurant du Val Fleurie in Livedun, this Michelin star restaurant was in the middle of nowhere and yet we were full every night. Most customers had desserts as they were simply luscious!

The pastry chef occupies a very special place in our kitchen and I hope I have included something for everyone here. My brother Dominique is a very gifted pastry chef. He is in the new generation of pastry chefs, using local ingredients and flavours and together we have developed several recipes with stunning results some of which are featured in this chapter. You may like to note that we have also had the odd disaster!

When I return home I always plan my trip with 3 important factors. First trout fishing in the Vosges mountain, second a trip to the stade Marcel Picot, our local football team and third a day at my brother's boulangerie patisserie. Spending the day and often the night there is an overwhelming experience as I often bring ingredients and recipes from Yorkshire which he then in return helps me develop some of our biggest sellers back in our restaurant in England, breads, tarte aux citron, black cherry and almond tart etc. have all been perfected with the help of my brother.

We both have an incredible satisfaction of opening in the morning with the sweet smell of warm bread spreading across the town square; even with 600 miles between us I can simply close my eyes and imagine the wonderful aroma from his bakery!

Pate a choux
Choux pastry

This makes 400g of pastry. Choux pastry can sometimes be difficult to get right but this recipe is easy and the result is simply brilliant.

5tbs of milk

5tbs of water

2tbs sweetened condensed milk

Half tsp of salt

70g unsalted butter

85g of plain flour

3 medium free range eggs

1. Put the milk, water, condensed milk, salt and butter into a medium sauce pan
2. Heat until butter has melted
3. Sieve the flour
4. Bring the liquid to the boil
5. Remove from the heat, then add the flour
6. Stir well with a wooden spoon, until the mixture becomes one
7. Leave to cool for 10 minutes
8. In a separate bowl place 3 eggs and whisk for 3 minutes until the eggs are lightly frothy
9. Add the mixture with the equivalent of one egg at a time
10. Beat the mixture well until it has absorbed the egg
11. Continue until all the eggs are in the mixture
12. Leave to rest for fifteen minutes
13. Then you simply shape the pastry as you wish choux, éclairs etc.
14. Preheat the oven to 180°C then cook for 20 minutes or until the choux are golden brown

Pate sucree
Sweet pastry

This makes 1 kilo of pastry and you can easily divide this into three, wrap well in cling film and freeze the rest for your next diner party. You can also flavour the pastry with cocoa powder.
As it is a delicate pastry the less you touch it with your hands the better as often when making pastries by hand, as you knead hard your hands gets hotter resulting in a warm slightly discoloured pastry. Use a electric blender as this is fast and effective.

The choice of ingredient is vital for the success of this recipe:

Flour:
At Mirabelle we use 2 types of flour for our recipes. For cakes and pastries we use organic plain flour type 45 and for breads we use plain and brown flour type 55.

Sugars:
We use caster sugar or icing sugar for pastries.

Fat:
We use unsalted butter. For best results leave the butter out of the fridge for at least three hours before using.

250g unsalted butter

180g icing sugar

2 vanilla pods

3 medium free range eggs

500g of organic plain flour

1. Place the butter and sugar in the bowl
2. Blend until smooth and creamy
3. Cut the vanilla pod in half and scrape the seeds into the mixture
4. Gently add each egg to the mixture and blend
5. Gradually add the flour, then blend again until the mixture becomes firm and crumbly
6. Remove from the blender then knead gently into a ball. Avoid overworking the pastry
7. Leave to rest for 30 minutes
8. Softly roll out the pastry

Tarte aux cerises noir et amandes
Black cherry and almond tart

Serves 6   Level 1

600g of sweet pastry

6 individual 8 centimetres moulds or a 30 centimetre tart mould

200g of fresh black Cherrie if in season or s tin of pitted black cherry will do

200g unsalted butter - leave to soften for at least 2 hours

200g caster sugar

200g ground almond

50g plain flour

3 medium eggs

1tbs organic almond essence

2tbs of orange marmalade or apricot jam

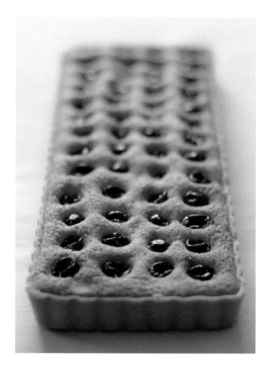

1. Preheat oven to 170°C
2. Line your mould with sweet pastry
3. Place in the fridge for 30 minutes to rest
4. Place the butter and sugar in a medium size mixing bowl
5. Using electric blender mix well until smooth and creamy
6. Add the flour, almond essence then blend well
7. Add the eggs and almond at the same time
8. Again blend well until smooth
9. Take the moulds out of the fridge
10. Using a table spoon carefully place the mixture in the mould three quarters full
11. Make sure you place the mixture in the middle of the mould then work your way gently to the side
12. Place the cherries in the mixture making sure they are pushed in well
13. Bake in a preheated oven for 20 to 25 minutes at 170°C
14. Once baked, leave to cool
15. Melt the marmalade gently in a microwave or in a pan on the stove
16. Brush the top of the tart with the marmalade until glazed
17. Serve warm with cream or vanilla ice cream

Cheesecake au toblerone
Toblerone cheesecake

You need to do this at least six hours prior to dinner or simply leave overnight.

Toblerone cheesecake is a favourite at the restaurant; we simply could not remove it from our menu without an outcry from our regulars. We use chocolate biscuits for our base but you could try ginger biscuits or almond biscuits which really work well with lemon or strawberry cheesecake.

This is an unbaked cheesecake but we are not using gelatine. You will need an 8" or 25cm non-stick tin with removable bottom for this recipe.

250g chocolate digestive biscuit
   or plain if you prefer
130g unsalted butter
160g icing sugar
500g cream cheese
400ml double cream
1tsp of vanilla extract
200g of Toblerone

1. Melt the unsalted butter slowly in a small pan on a low flame
2. Crush the biscuits in a blender (or in a plastic bag with a rolling pin)
3. Combine the biscuit crumbs with the butter then press into the tin
4. Chill until firm
5. In a large mixing bowl place the cream cheese, the icing sugar and the vanilla extract
6. Beat well until smooth
7. Leave to rest whilst you whip the cream until soft peak
8. Fold the cream into the cream cheese then pour the mixture onto the biscuit base, smooth the mixture well making sure you leave 2cm space to add the Toblerone
9. Leave in the fridge overnight
10. Place the Toblerone in a mixing bowl over boiling water
11. Add 2tbs of brandy or baileys
12. Add 2tbs of water
13. Stir until melted
14. Pour the Toblerone mixture onto the cheesecake
15. Leave to rest for at least 2 hours

Tips:

To make it easier to remove, if you have a blowtorch, gently warm the side of the mould. When cutting portions use a jug of warm water to dip your knife into after each slice so you get a perfect cut don't forget to wipe your knife after each dip too.

Tarte au citron
Lemon tart
Serve 6   Level 1

My brother's recipe... many thanks Dominique.

Dominique and I have followed similar careers. Although we operate in different countries our passion for flavours have remained a vocation and at times an obsession, the internet allows us to communicate our perfected recipes from a distance. When I visit France we often spend our evenings until the early hours of the morning exchanging ideas and recipes.

This recipe is a perfect example of our working together. There are two ways you can make a tarte au citron, both very good, basically think sweet, crumbling pastry filled with a rich lemon custard.

Recipe 1

For the pastry case:

1. Line your mould well with 400g of sweet pastry
2. Place tin foil and beans onto the pastry to stop it from bubbling
3. Tip: you don't need to buy ceramic baking beans as they are often quite expensive just buy a bag of dried chick peas it is a brilliant and cheap option which you can use over and over again
4. Bake for 10-15 minutes at 180°C or until the pastry is cooked and pale golden
5. Remove from the oven then leave to cool for 15 minutes

The lemon mixture:

2 eggs
50g caster sugar
175ml of double cream
Juice and zest of 3 lemons

1. Whisk the egg and the caster sugar, add the cream and the lemon zest, juice
2. Mix well
3. Pour into the cooked pastry case
4. Cook for around 30 minutes at 165°C
5. Leave to cool for at least 4 hours before serving

Recipe 2:

Serves 6   Level 1

For this recipe you will need to bake blind (pastry is baked before being filled) using a 25cm shallow tart mould.

For the pastry case:

1. Line your mould well with 400g of sweet pastry
2. Place tin foil and beans onto the pastry to stop it from bubbling
3. Bake for 10-15 minutes at 180°C or until the pastry is cooked and pale golden
4. Remove from the oven then leave to cool for 15 minutes

The lemon mixture - prepare the night before:

500ml of freshly squeezed lemon juice for best result

200g of unsalted butter

200g caster sugar

10 medium eggs

1. Place the lemon juice, butter and sugar in a large saucepan
2. Bring the mixture to a gentle boil stirring well until all melted
3. Break the eggs into a medium bowl whisk firmly
4. Remove the mixture from the heat for 5 minutes
5. Then add the beaten eggs to the warm mixture
6. Bring back to a gentle boil for 2 minutes, whisking constantly
7. Remove from the heat and immediately place mixture into a container
8. Place in fridge over night

On the day:

1. Place the empty pastry case onto the dish you intend to serve the tart from, (when you have added the mixture to the pastry you will not be able to move it).
2. Pour the mixture into the empty pastry case using a spoon to smooth it evenly
3. Thinly slice 2 lemons
4. Place lemon slices around the edge of the pastry
5. Finish with icing sugar and strawberry for colour

Tarte aux pommes et poires
Apple and pear tart

Serves 6   Level 2

A sweet pastry case with an overflowing mix of caramelised fruits and nuts is a great dessert with a brilliant look.

Tip: Though you can use almost any type of apples and pears for this recipe, I have found certain varieties to be juicer and sweeter than others; for apples look out for Cox orange pippin, Russet and Braeburn. For pears consider William, Conference or Conice.

For the pastry case:
400g of sweet pastry
For this recipe you will need to bake blind pastry using a 25 cm shallow tart mould

For the apple filling:
2 large cooking apple
50g sugar
1 vanilla pod
50g butter

1. Peel and chop the apple in a medium saucepan
2. add the sugar, butter and vanilla pod
3. cook gently for 20 minutes
4. leave to cool down

For the fruit and nut filling (the nuts are optional in case you have any allergies)

3 desert apples

3 desert pears

50g butter

50g sugar

1tbs honey

50g almonds

50g pistachio

50g good quality dried mixed fruit

Pastry case:

1. Line your mould well with the sweet pastry
2. Place tin foil and beans onto the pastry to stop it from bubbling
3. Bake for 10-15 minutes at 180°C or until the pastry is cooked and pale golden
4. Cover with a tea towel then leave it out over night

For the filling:

1. Peel the apples and pears
2. Cut into equal cubes around 1cm
3. Pour into a large frying pan the sugar, butter and honey bring this to the boil until you reach a light caramelised colour
4. Add the apple and pears cook for 5 minutes again gently
5. Add the nuts then cook for a further 5 minutes making sure that all the cubes of fruit and nuts are coated with the caramel honey
6. Remove from the heat then pour the apple filling in the pastry case smooth out evenly
7. The pour the fruit and nut filling onto the apple filling
8. Smooth out the filling evenly with a spoon
9. Serve warm or cold with cream or ice cream

Mousse au chocolat noir et blanc, tuile a la noix de coco
Black and white chocolate mousse with coconut tuile

Serve 6   Level 1

This is the easiest chocolate mousse in the world for which you will need 6 tall glasses for this recipe as you will apply layers of chocolate mousse.

Place the 6 tall glasses on a tray in the fridge.

For the coconut tuile:

2 egg whites
75g icing sugar
65g grated coconut
50g unsalted butter

1. In a large mixing bowl whisk the egg whites until smooth
2. Gently stir in the sugar and the coconut
3. Gently add the melted butter to the mixture
4. Pour the mixture into a greaseproof baking tray
5. Chill for one hour
6. Bake for 3 minutes at 160°C
7. Remove from the oven and whilst still warm use a small pastry cutter to stamp out biscuits to the size and shape you want
8. Leave to cool

For the dark chocolate mousse:

200g good quality dark chocolate

250ml of double cream

4tbs of Baileys

1. Melt the chocolate in a mixing bowl over boiling water
2. Stir in the 2tbs of baileys
3. Leave to cool whilst you whisk the double cream to a hard peak
4. Gently fold the almost cold chocolate into the cream
   (Make sure the chocolate is not too hot as the cream will simply melt)
5. Set aside whilst you make the white chocolate mousse

For the white chocolate mousse:

200g good quality white chocolate

250ml double cream

2tbs white rum

Strawberries to decorate

Use the same process as for the dark chocolate mousse

To serve:

1. Spoon dark chocolate into a tall glass making sure you do not touch the side
2. Then spoon on the white chocolate mousse
3. Carry on the process until the glass is three quarters full
4. Finish the dish with placing a couple of strawberry's on top
5. Then place 2 coconut tuile on the side of each glass

Tarte aux pommes
Apple tart
Serves 6   Level 1

Every French restaurant has apple tart on its desserts menu. With numerous variations everyone has the perfect one and here is mine! It is quick, easy and it looks great.

For the pastry:
175g plain flour
pinch of salt
125g butter
1 egg yolk
3tbs cold water

For the frangipane:
125g butter, softened
100g caster sugar
1 beaten egg
1 egg yolk
1tbs Calvados or Kirsch
2tbs plain flour
100g ground almonds

Additional ingredients:
3 to 4 ripe dessert apples - peeled, cored, halved and thinly sliced
5tbs apricot jam

To make the pâtebrisée:

1. Stir together the flour and salt
2. Add butter, egg yolk, and water and mix until the mixture forms large crumbs. (if the crumbs are too dry, add a little more water)
3. Press the crumbs firmly together to make a dough, it should be soft but not sticky.
4. Press the dough into a ball and wrap it in a plastic bag or cling film. Chill for at least 30 minutes or until firm. (The dough can be stored in the fridge for up to 3 days)
5. To make the frangipane, cream together the butter and 100g of sugar in a medium bowl until light and soft. Gradually mix in the egg and the remaining egg yolk one at a time.
6. Stir in the Calvados or Kirsch. Add 2tbs of flour to the ground almonds, then mix this into the batter and set aside.
7. Roll the pastry dough to a 30cm circle on a lightly floured surface. Fold loosely into quarters, and centre the point in a 10 inch tart or pie pan. Unfold dough, and press into the bottom and up the sides. Prick all over with a fork, and flute the edges. Return pastry to the refrigerator to chill until firm.
8. Preheat the oven to 200°C. Place a baking tray inside the oven while it preheats.
9. Spoon the frangipane into the chilled pastry, and spread into an even layer. Arrange the apple slices in an overlapping spiral pattern. Each slice should have one edge pressed into the frangipane until it touches the pastry base, and then overlap the previous slice. Start at the outside edge, and work towards the centre.
10. Place the tart onto the warm baking tray and bake until the frangipane begins to brown (15-20 minutes). Then reduce the heat to 180°C and bake for another 15-20 minutes.
11. Ten minutes before the end, sprinkle the tart with sugar then continue to cook for the remainder of the time.
12. Transfer to a wire rack to cool.
13. A short time before serving, warm the apricot jam and brush on top for a nice glaze. (You may need to add some water if necessary to make it a liquid consistency).

Soupe aux fraises
Strawberry soup
Croutons de meringues
Meringue croutons
Crème a la menthe
Minted cream
Serves 4   Level 1

This is a great summer desert but you can also serve it as a starter on a hot summer evening. June marks the start of the British strawberry season but it is at its peak at the end of July. In terms of flavour, English strawberries are so much better than the ghastly imported berries which are typically piled high at 'two for the price of one' at this time of year and which taste more of straw than berry. It is worth waiting for!

This recipe is the result of several trial and errors in my brother's patisserie in France, as he was preparing strawberry tart I simply started to mix flavours and after several examples here is the result.

1kg of good quality strawberry
4tbs of grenadine syrup or strawberry syrup
4tbs crème de cassis
4tbs of grand Marnier
100g caster sugar
1 lemon juice
2 meringues
100ml of double cream
Mint leaves

1. Wash and dry the strawberries then cut them into quarters
2. Place in a medium size bowl
3. Add the grenadine syrup, grand Marnier and crème de cassis, sugar and lemon juice
4. Stir well and leave in the fridge until ready to serve
5. You can make the meringue or simply purchase from good food outlets
6. In a mixing bowl place the cream and whip to medium firm
7. Chop the mint leaves and add to the cream folding gently at that point
8. Place the soup in a chilled soup bowl
9. Spoon on a dollop of cream and finish with meringues on the side

Ananas tarte tatin, glace a la noix de coco
Caramelised pineapple tart tatin with coconut ice cream
Serves 4   Level 1

This recipe has a Caribbean feel as over the last few years I have tried to mix Caribbean flavours and old fashioned French classical.

1 large ripe pineapple
400g puff pastry
200g caster sugar
25g butter
4 scoops of vanilla ice cram
200g grated coconut
6tbs Malibu

1. Using a sharp knife peel the pineapple from its hard skin removing all the black bits that are often encrusted in the fruit and cut 4 slices about 2cm thick
2. Remove the centre with a small cutter
3. Place the sugar in a frying pan and cook slowly until the sugar is golden brown
4. Place the pineapple slices in the caramel and cook slowly for 2 minutes each side
5. Place the pineapple on a buttered baking tray
6. Place 25g of butter in the caramel together with 4tbs of malibu, cook for one minute and pour over the pineapple
7. Roll the puff pastry quite thin and with the help of a large cutter or simply a saucer cut 4 circles of pastry making sure to cover the pineapple fully
8. Brush the pasty with butter and bake for 20 minutes at 180°C

The ice cream:

1. Place the shredded coconut in a small tray
2. Scoop 4 large spoons of vanilla ice cream and drop it into the coconut
3. Roll well until covered
4. Place in the freezer until later
5. Reheat the pineapple tatin if necessary
8. Place the tatin on the plate with the coconut ice cream on top
9. Optionally decorate with a sugar basket
9. Serve immediately

Crème brulee a la rubarbe
Crème brulee with rhubarb compote

Serves 6   Level 3

Crème Brûlée is one of those classic French desserts that can be altered according to the seasons and fruits. The qualities of the ingredients are vital to the success of this dish. Of course Yorkshire is renowned for growing rhubarb and it is worth getting organised and handpicking the necessary ingredients.

Vanilla pod - pods from Madagascar are the best and will give you maximum flavour. Try purchasing the ones in a glass or plastic tube or vac pac as it will keep the beans moist and maintain flavour.
Double cream - extra thick cream is better than regular.
Sugar - use brown Demerara or Muscovado as they have a strong flavour and good for the topping too.
Eggs - medium free range eggs are perfect for this dish.

I would advise that if you add a fruit compote to enhance the dish then simply serve it separately rather than inside the brulee as often fruits create unnecessary moisture and may dilute the mixture.

I think the easiest and possibly least stressful way to caramelise the topping is with a blowtorch. However, as most people don't own one, and calling out the plumber at nine in the evening could prove a tad expensive, just place the sugared puddings under a very hot pre-heated grill until golden and bubbling (though watch them like a hawk). Remember to leave the desserts to rest for a while in order to let the sugar harden and the ramekins cool down.

500ml double cream

1 fat juicy vanilla pod

100g brown sugar (plus extra for the topping)

3 egg yolks

2 whole eggs

200g of rhubarb

The rhubarb:

1. Carefully peel the rhubarb and cut into small cubes
2. In a medium pan add 20g of butter and the rhubarb
3. Bring to a gentle simmer and cook for 5 minutes
4. Leave to cool then place in the fridge over night

The crème brulee:

1. Pre-heat oven to 140C°
2. Pour the cream into a saucepan. Split the vanilla pod lengthways and scrape the seeds into the cream. Chop the empty pod into bits and add these too. Bring to boiling point, turn off the heat and cover with a lid. Leave to infuse for five to ten minutes.
3. Beat the sugar and the eggs together in a large heat-proof bowl until pale and creamy. Bring the cream back to a boiling point, then pour over the egg mixture, whisking all the time until thickened - (you should have a smooth custard like the consistency of double cream - a grainy texture means it's been over-cooked and you'll have to start over again).
4. Strain through a fine sieve into a large jug, use this to fill 6 ramekins about two thirds full.
5. Place the ramekins in a large roasting tray and pour in enough hot water to come halfway up their sides. Place on the centre shelf, bake for 40 minutes to one hour, or until the custards are just set and still a bit wobbly in the middle.
6. Remove from the water and allow to cool to room temperature.

Weights

Metric	imperial
5g	1/8 oz
10g	1/4oz
15g	1/2oz
20g	3/4oz
25g	1oz
50g	2oz
85g	3oz
100g	3 1/2 oz
115g	4oz
140g	5oz
175g	6oz
200g	7oz
225g	8oz
250g	9oz
280g	10oz
315g	11oz
350g	12oz
400g	14oz
450g	1lb
500g	1lb 2oz
600g	1lb 5oz
800g	1lb 12oz
900g	2lb
1kg	2lb 4oz
1.5kg	3lb 5oz
2kg	4lb 8oz

Oven temperature

Celcius	Fahrenheit	Gas	Description
110°C	225°F	1/2	COOL
120°C	250°F	1/2	COOL
140°C	275°F	1	VERY LOW
150°C	300°F	2	VERY LOW
160°C	325°F	3	LOW
180°C	350°F	4	MODERATE
190°C	375°F	5	HOT
200°C	400°F	6	HOT
220°C	425°F	7	VERY HOT
230°C	450°F	8	VERY HOT

Liquid equivalent

1 tablespoon	15ml
2fl oz	60ml
3fl oz	100ml
4fl oz	125ml
5fl oz	150ml
6fl oz	180ml
7fl oz	200ml
8fl oz	250ml
10fl oz (½ pint)	300ml
12fl oz	375ml
15fl oz (¾ pint)	500ml
1pint	600ml
1 ¾ pint	1litre